THE BODY LANGUAGE OF POKER

MIKE CARO'S
Book of Tells

THE BODY LANGUAGE OF POKER

MIKE CARO'S
Book of Tells

By Mike Caro
"The Mad Genius"

A GAMBLING TIMES BOOK
DISTRIBUTED BY CAROL PUBLISHING GROUP

Carol Publishing Group Edition - 1994

Senior Editor: Jerrold Kazdoy
Art Direction: Mark Fichera

Manufactured in the United States of America
ISBN: 0-89746-100-2

Distributed by Carol Publishing Group
120 Enterprise Avenue
Secaucus, N.J. 07094

Carol Publishing Group books are available at special discounts for bulk purchases, for sales promotions, fund raising, or educational purposes. Special editions can also be created to specifications. For details contact: Special Sales Department, Carol Publishing Group, 120 Enterprise Ave., Secaucus, NJ 07094

10 9 8 7 6 5 4 3 2 1

Library of Congress Cataloging-in-Publication Data

Caro, Mike.
  The body language of poker : Mike Caro's book of tells / by Mike Caro
      p.   cm.
  "A Citadel Press book."
    1. Poker--Psychological aspects. 2. Nonverbal communication
  (Psychology)   I. Title : Book of tells.
  GV1255.P78C37   1994
  795.41'2--dc20   93-45561
                                                           CIP

All material presented in this book is offered as information to the reader. No inducement to gamble is intended or implied.

A NOTE FROM THE PUBLISHER

As the publisher of Gambling Times Incorporated, including all of our periodicals and books, it is my privilege and responsibility to read everything before it goes to the printer for publication. Occasionally I have to reject passages, articles and even entire book manuscripts because they may contain libelous or incorrect data, false assumptions, or offensive material. Therefore, I read all material before the public sees it, sometimes several months in advance. The publication of this book represented a significant personal edge that I gained over the poker playing public. In the few weeks before publication, I used this book to gain a significant advantage at the poker tables of Las Vegas and Southern California. In some cases, it was like taking candy from a baby. The other players could just as well have shown me their hands. They exhibited so many tells that I never understood in previous sessions at the tables. Before this book, I was a somewhat better than average poker player. . . . Now I'm ready for major league tournaments.

Stanley R. Sludikoff

About the Author

For five years Mike Caro has clarified and pioneered some of the most important gambling concepts ever put on paper. He is consultant to many of the world's leading poker players and his advice on casino games and gambling in general is highly regarded throughout the world.

Caro is primarily known as a teacher and theorist, but beyond that—twice world poker champion Doyle Brunson calls him "the best draw poker player alive."

His in-depth statistics on poker and gambling are among the most widely quoted today. Caro is a computer wizard who uses his exclusive programs to back up his research. In addition, he is famous for his work on the psychology and philosophy of gambling.

In 1983 Caro gave a paid seminar at the Bingo Palace in Las Vegas and drew 158 people, many traveling from out of state to hear his two-hour lecture on poker. At full-scale gambling-related seminars, he draws audiences who pay as much as $195.

Caro is known as *"The Mad Genius,"* and for good reason. Much of his teaching is unconventional and very profound. Yet he explains things in crisp, clear language that will have your pulse racing as you learn the secret keys to winning.

Photo by Lee McDonald

Photo 1: "Mad Genius" Mike Caro leans on the poker table during one of six *tells* photo sessions. In all, more than 100 players, managers, experts and casino employees contributed to the making of *Mike Caro's Book of Tells*. This photo session was held at the Palace Station (formerly the Bingo Palace) in Las Vegas. Poker room manager Steve Schlemmer is at right.

Photo 2: Caro addresses the largest paid audience (158) that ever gathered for a one-man poker seminar. The subject of his lecture, given at the Palace Station in Las Vegas, was "All-Tells, Only-Tells."

Table of Contents

Foreword

By
David M. Hayano, Ph.D.

> *David Hayano is Professor of Anthropology at California State University, Northridge. Among his published works is* Poker Faces *(see Note 2 at the end of this foreword). The acclaimed and often-quoted book was the culmination of several years of interviews, observation and research which allowed Hayano to define poker lifestyles in astonishing detail. He is also widely regarded as a world-class poker player.*

I was delighted when Mike Caro asked me to write the foreword to this book. Over the past ten years I have played poker with—I should say *against*—Caro in countless sessions from lowball to hold 'em, battling heads-up and in full games. These numerous confrontations have convinced me of his authoritative knowledge of poker and his uncanny ability to "read" his opponents. And, unfortunately for his tablemates, Caro himself is virtually "tell-less." He is almost impossible to read accurately. Once you think you have him he is likely to show you a big hand. Then when you think you've made a good judgment laydown against him, he is just as prone to spread a complete bust under your nose. There is no doubt that Caro's expertise stretches beyond his acclaimed work on poker strategy and statistics. He is highly qualified to write this book and is able to teach his lessons well.

For nearly a century, poker manuals of the "how to play and win" variety have consisted mainly of various low-level basic strategies, practical advice, and a few statistical tables thrown in for good measure. It is my opinion that most of these poker books have been repetitive and unoriginal. Until recently a fresh approach to the game has been hard to find.[1] But now, by focusing on one aspect of the game, albeit a complex and fascinating one at that, we have entered new ground.

We must first see that everything poker players do while sitting at the table—betting, checking, calling, raising, bluffing—involves movement

xiii

or behavior of one kind or another. Furthermore, we can assume that poker behavior is indicative of mood or emotion, and that players may reveal their hidden, internal psychological states by how they act. For example, bluffing can be considered to be a kind of nonverbal lying, one which many poker players do not always carry off successfully. Like a verbal lie, they are found out and must pay the penalties. We are then ready to allow for the fact that in the study of poker behavior, various "mistakes" or "clues" may be found.

It is quite obvious that noting how one's opponents behave is a crucial part of being a perceptive and winning poker player. But, amazingly, time after time I have seen many poker players—indeed, the majority of players—completely disregard what their opponents do! These oblivious players are "ego-centric." Their only shortsighted concern is what they have in their hands, and what action they will take in the next few seconds. This is a fatal flaw, and most professional poker players will tell you that poker is perhaps the ultimate game of human interaction and behavior.

Through the analysis of tells we are trying to understand how players behave and what this reveals about their motivation. One of the first steps in discovering tells is for a player to develop a sense of the *baseline behavioral repertoire* of one's opponents. Is he generally a calm, meek bettor, or is he normally wild and aggressive? What is his usual, consistent pattern of play?

Some tells are clearly obvious. Many amateur players literally cannot control themselves emotionally when they have a lock hand or miss yet another flush or straight or lowball draw. In the first case, their anxiety and enthusiasm are apparent: They sit forward, grab a stackful of chips, and ask loudly, "How much is it to me?" In the second instance, when they have missed a hand, they slump down in their chairs, flick the edge of their cards impatiently and mutter under their breath. No special trained observational skills are required to spot these players.

Although more experienced players are less obvious and have fewer tells, many of them, too, may leak about their deception in predictable ways. I have found that many experienced players, including professionals, tend foremost to do the "opposite" of what their baseline pattern suggests. For example, a weak player who suddenly bets strongly, and a wild, gesturing player who puts in a timid bet, are quite likely to be "lying" about their hands. This *rule of opposites* applies quite nicely for most average players.

Unfortunately, the most experienced poker players tend to be more complex behaviorally. They cannot be read literally. Sometimes they may deliberately act the opposite of their standard pattern and other times they will not. But still, tells are discernible if one looks carefully at the entire context and flow of behavior. How were the chips thrown in? Where were they placed? Was the bet fast or slow? Is the player looking off to the side or at the chips in the pot?

Moreover, other factors (which cannot be photographed) are important: Is the player winning or losing at the moment? Is he on tilt? Is he ready to leave the game or has he just arrived?

Again, by cataloging the baseline behavioral repertoire of individual players, one can begin to recognize "deviations" from normal patterns and develop a second sense, a "feel" for something not being entirely correct. In any case a novice poker player, or an experienced poker player who enters a new game with unknown opponents, should use his calls as a kind of behavioral experiment. You have paid not only to see a hand, but you have paid to see the *quality* of the hand and how it was played. Indeed, every poker hand should be seen this way. Professionals will tell you that one must watch the game intently, whether you are involved in the pot or not. When a fellow player has made a good or bad call, you can benefit from this. You have been treated to a free experiment. You have paid nothing but can profit immensely from it.

Finding one's own tells is not so easy. You can ask a friend to observe your play and then to try to discover leaks in your play. Another test can be applied: If few of your bluffs are successful and you are rarely called with a good hand then something is amiss. Your maximum potential is not being extracted. Your play is either too predictable or too telltale.

As a professional behavioral scientist whose primary interest is the study of human behavior, the analysis of tells is particularly pertinent to me because it is a domain of research that is just beginning to gain the special attention it deserves. The ivory towers of academe and the green-felt tables of poker cardrooms are not as far apart as one might think. For years poker players have known about and discussed matters such as deception and tells amongst themselves, but it has been only within the last few decades that social scientists have begun to investigate this subject matter for themselves. Here it seems reasonable to assume that poker behavior can be subsumed and analyzed as a subclass of behavior in general, and that the findings of social science might be extremely valuable in future studies of poker players.[2] As evidence, an increasing number of scholarly papers on deception, lying and distorted communication have begun to appear. Yet most of this research is still entirely theoretical and experimental. What is lacking is practicality and application to the "real world" (including poker tables) of ordinary people and gamesmen. To be sure, experienced poker players, with their practical expertise in their special arena of knowledge, have much to offer the social scientist.

Eventually what I hope to see is a merging between the theories and findings of behavioral science and its practical application to everyday life. The study of tells is a perfect bridge for this synthesis, for it represents a kind of behavior that is both observable and repetitive.[3]

In any analysis the first procedure must be to observe, classify, and arrange and rearrange what has been observed. Most tells involve only microseconds of behavior, but if these are our only clues to what is going on, then let us take up the challenge and observe others *and* ourselves more closely.

The practical advantages of spotting tells is obvious: Your poker skills and monetary gains will increase dramatically. With *Mike Caro's Book of Tells* in hand, a truly original book in its field, we can finally get a glimpse of the ways by which we can sort out the hard-to-read liars and bluffers across the table from our other more predictable foes. We are on our first step in poker toward being able to determine the truth.

As a major step in the cataloging, explanation and pictorial description of tells, this book is essential for all poker players. With it we are finally beginning to see that successful poker playing involves a complexity and multiplicity of human verbal and nonverbal actions. Like a puzzling design on a tapestry we must begin to separate the individual strands of movement and gesture, and work toward discovering the structure of lies and tells.

NOTES

1. A notable exception is the compendium by Doyle Brunson and his collaborators, *Super/System—A Course in Power Poker,* Las Vegas: B and G Publishing Company, 1978.

2. I have attempted to do this in my book, *Poker Faces: The Life and Work of Professional Card Players,* Berkeley: University of California Press, 1982.

3. See, for example, my more detailed papers: "Poker Lies and Tells," *Human Behavior* 8(3):18-22, 1979; and especially, "Communicative Competency Among Poker Players," *Journal of Communication* 30(2):113-120, 1980.

Introduction

I'll make this short so we can look at the pictures.

Much of my published poker research has been statistical. Even at seminars, I teach tactics based largely on mathematical concepts. However, recent scientific studies analyzing the brain tissue of dead poker players proved the following:

22% of winning is mathematics;

3% of winning is intuition;

8% of winning is luck;

15% of winning is discipline;

52% of winning is psychology.

What fascinated me most about that study (first published, I think, in the *Enquirer*), was the 52% of winning attributed to psychology. Golly, that's one percent for every card in the deck!

Hey, it's too early in the morning to be silly, so let's talk straight. Once you've mastered the basic elements of a winning poker formula, psychology becomes the key ingredient separating break-even players from world-class superstars. The most profitable kind of poker psychology is the ability to read your opponents. Look closely and you'll see opponents giving away the strength of their hands just by their mannerisms.

Any mannerism which helps you determine the secrets of an opponent's hand is called a *tell*. Until a few years ago, nobody understood tells thoroughly. Experienced players would try to uncover trends in their opponents' behavior. Maybe they discovered that one opponent would always loosen his tie five minutes before attempting a major bluff. Such discoveries are important, but there's a much better way to go about reading opponents.

A very powerful method is contained in this book.

If you wanted to catalog all the possible tells an opponent might exhibit, the list might go on forever. You could sit for a few days and jot down several thousand things that opponents might do under stress.

Unfortunately, after all that work, your list would be pitifully incomplete. There are millions of tells you could write down if you could only think of them all.

There is a simple way to read your opponents. You must learn the motives behind their actions. Then, even when you encounter a tell you've never seen before, you'll have a good idea of what it means. When you're finished with this book, you won't have to memorize all the actions of each opponent. Instead, you'll be able to fit their mannerisms into universal categories of tells. You'll often know exactly what they hold and, better still, you'll know *why* they're acting as they are. You'll get deep inside their minds. And sometimes you'll be positive what cards an opponent holds—just as if he'd turned his hand face up on the table!

When you can do that, your profits will soar. In my opinion, a conscientious winner will at least triple his profits once he masters the science of tells.

It's important that you comprehend the reason why many tells happen. Most tells occur because players are trying to conceal the true strength of their hands. The most likely way they attempt to do this is to act in a manner that will convey the *opposite* of what they're holding. If a hand is weak, they'll try to convince you it's strong. If a hand is strong, they'll try to convince you it's weak. In this sense, your opponents are actors.

This brings us to. . .

Caro's Great Law of Tells

Players are either acting or they aren't. If they are acting, then decide what they want you to do and disappoint them.

The tells discussed in this book follow a disciplined format. It looks like this...

Photo

Title:

Category:

Description:

Motivation:

Reliability: Weak players =   %
                    Average players =   %
                    Strong players =   %

Value Per Hour: $1 limit = $
                        $10 limit = $
                      $100 limit = $

Discussion:

Best Strategy:

First study the photo(s) referred to in the **Photo** heading. **Title** is just a short label to give you an idea of what the tell is about. **Category** provides the type of tell. **Description** explains what the photos show. The player's reason for acting the way he does is given after **Motivation. Reliability** is a rough educated guess, based on several studies and much personal judgment, that shows how often a tell is likely to be accurate. **Value Per Hour** provides a very rough figure of how much the tell is worth to you in various size games. The assumption is that you're playing against mostly weak-to-average opponents. **Discussion** provides more insight into the tell. **Best Strategy** tells you what to do.

An important thing to keep in mind is that **Reliability** does not need to be, and seldom is, 100%. Tells give you indications which you should balance against all other factors. For instance, if you get a medium-strong tell that your opponent is bluffing, *but he never bluffs,* you have a problem. You should give value to the fact that an opponent never bluffs, but you should also give value to the fact that he seems to be bluffing. One thing that's for certain: He's *more likely* to be bluffing when you see the tell than when you don't. To be successful at the science of tells, you must always rate the **Reliability** in relation to the situation at hand. It's interesting to note that a tell does not need to be even 50% accurate to be of value! Suppose the pot were $400 and it cost you only $100 to call. Suppose further that you could beat a bluff and *only* a bluff. If this situation occurred five times and you called every time, you'd need to catch your opponent bluffing only once to break even. That's because you'd lose $100 four times (total $400) and once you'd win the $400 that's in the pot. In other words, you'd need to win only 20% of the time. Then, if a tell led you to believe there were a 40% chance your opponent were bluffing, it would certainly be worth a call.

Some tells are nearly 100% accurate. Others are simply powerful clues you should use along with other factors to make your decision.

Before we get started, I want to thank some of those who contributed most to the making of this book.

For lending their expertise: Doyle Brunson, Bobby Baldwin, Tom McEvoy, Jack Straus, Michael Wiesenberg, John Fox, Victor Resnick, Steve Margulies and particularly Rick Greider.

For technical support and advice: Stanley Sludikoff, Len Miller, Tom Bowling, Arnold Abrams, Jerrold Kazdoy and Steve Steinkamp.

For photography: Cliff Stanley, Lee McDonald, Frank Mitrani, Raiko Hartman and Allen Photographers of Las Vegas.

For other important contributions: Chip Johnson, Rosemary Dufault, Eloise Nudelman, Arthur Sathmary, Mason Malmuth, David Sklansky and Jerry Weinstein.

Most of those people offered direct contributions, while some (particularly Jack Straus, Bobby Baldwin and David Sklansky) gave useful information in the course of our conversations.

And especially I'd like to thank Phyllis Caro, who insisted that this work be finished without further delay and then made it happen.

The value you get out of this book is up to you. The more you study these tells and try to find them in your own poker games, the more successful you'll become. But be patient and let the tells speak for themselves. The most dangerous thing you can do is to imagine a tell that doesn't exist. Most people would rather call than throw a hand away. For that reason, it's human nature to seek tells that allow you to call. Some students of mine have tended to neglect tells which indicate they should pass a hand they would normally play.

Keep a cool, disinterested attitude. You should be as eager to find a reason to pass as you should be to call. Concentrate and let the tells talk.

When you graduate from this tells course, you'll know for sure why this man...

Photo by Lee McDonald

Photo 3: . . . is never as much of a threat. . .

Continued

Photo by Lee McDonald

Photo 4: . . . as this man.

Tell Stars

Here is a complete list of the *Book of Tells* cast. Most stars appear more than once. The photograph referred to is one place where the model can be seen. Thanks to all.

Among the Tell Stars are more than two dozen world-class players, notably Chip Johnson (famous poker theorist and teacher), Rick Greider (the world's foremost seven-stud expert), John Fox (author of the best-selling *Play Poker, Quit Work and Sleep Till Noon* and other books), Ron Faltinsky, Richard Green, Ray Noren (an authority on protecting players against cheaters) and David Heyden.

Additionally, there are four managers of major Las Vegas poker rooms: Steve Schlemmer (Palace Station, where many of the photographs were taken), Jan Bowman (Sam's Town), Don Maedgen (Four Queens) and John Sutton (Imperial Palace). Also modeling is Tom Bowling, who was formerly manager of the Palace Station poker room (then called the Bingo Palace) and is now both head of the sports book and Director of Casino Marketing.

Among the major poker journalists pictured are Tex Sheahan, Stuart M. Jacobs and Norman J. Bogart. LeRoy B. Merillat runs LeRoy's Sports Book in Las Vegas.

More than half the photos were taken at the Palace Station. Special thanks goes to the entire staff of that progressive poker room for its important contribution to the young science of tells. Many of the tells were staged at the Rainbow Club in Gardena, California, which suspended operations in 1983.

The Rainbow was among my favorite places to play, and its closing saddens me. One other sad thing before we get on with the happy magic of tells: Most of the photographs taken at the studios of Allen Photographers in Las Vegas were lost when that establishment was destroyed by fire in 1983. Only 12 photos survived out of more than 100. Fortunately, everyone who posed at the studios appears in this book. Those lost tells were later re-shot at the Palace Station.

Part One

Tells From Those
Who Are Unaware

When I get through with you, the magic of tells will be your key to profit for life. Most of your profit will come from reading players who are trying to deceive you. Those are actors who are aware of what they're doing. Usually they will act exactly opposite of the true strength of their cards. If their hands are hideous, they will try to make you think that they hold something fearsome. If their hands are powerful, they will try to convince you that they hold garbage. We'll get into the world of actors in *Part Two—Tells From Actors.*

Right now we'll deal in another important category of tells. The folks in the upcoming photos will give you valuable information, even though they *won't* be trying to fool you.

Although these tells are not from actors, these same people probably *will be* actors at other times. It's just that they aren't bothering to act at this particular moment. So let's see what they have to tell us . . .

Chapter 1

Noncombat Tells

While the majority of tells occur during the competition for a poker pot, there is some valuable information that can be learned about our opponents when they're not involved in a poker hand.

Poker tests our perception. It also tests our logic and our competitive instincts. In a sense it's a safe and sane form of warfare. Poker war is not only the competition for each pot, hand after hand. Poker war is bigger than just *hand-to-hand* combat, because there are important things happening *between* hands—things you should be observing.

Besides the noncombat tells illustrated in this section, you should notice things about each player's appearance that might provide clues to future poker behavior.

Specifically, well-dressed people tend to play conservatively. However, a man wearing a rumpled business suit with a loosened tie is probably in a gambling mood and will play looser than he would if that same suit were recently donned and his tie were in perfect position.

Poker authority John Fox claims that people wearing religious amulets are luck conscious, hard to bluff and play too many pots. Obviously the Reverend Fox means no disrespect with that theory, and there is probably truth in it. Certainly, players displaying good-luck charms or showing superstitious behavior tend to be more liberal with their poker dollars than average players.

Here are a few of my personal observations and those of my students. (Many of those students have been women and minorities, so in no sense are these comments intended as sexist, racist or unfriendly.) As a general rule, women are harder to bluff than men. Orientals are either very skillful or very luck oriented. Relatively few blacks play to win; most tend to gamble more liberally than other players. When you're up against an unknown player, you'll earn extra profit by assuming he or she will play as a stereotype until you learn differently.

Let's look at some noncombat tells...

Photo 5

Title: When I was a boy, I liked to play with blocks.

Category: Noncombat

Description: This man has gone out of his way to arrange his chips neatly. He's even bothered to line up the markings on the sides of the chips.

Motivation: His personality, either permanently or momentarily, is not very reckless. Neatly arranged chips make him feel secure.

Reliability:		
	Weak players	= 88%
	Average players	= 68%
	Strong players	= 59%

Value Per Hour:		
	$1 limit	= $0.33
	$10 limit	= $1.14
	$100 limit	= $3.15

Discussion: Very rarely is stacking chips used as a ploy by a player. Most players only bother to *act* when the rewards are immediate (i.e., a pot which is still being fought for). Glimpses of an opponent's true nature can often be gained by watching the way he stacks his chips. The very organized manner in which these chips are arranged suggests that this player will probably choose his hands carefully, seldom bluff and won't display a lot of gamble. Of course his mood may change during the game, but in that case his stacks will probably become less neatly arranged. Notice that there are a few extra chips on top of his large stacks. This could be his profit. That's important to know, because you can frequently bluff successfully just by betting slightly more than his profit. Players are reluctant to call when they're winning now, but would be losing if they made an unsuccessful call. Also, note that this fellow is very neatly attired. This is often, but not always, an indication of conservative play.

Best Strategy: Don't get involved with medium-strength hands after this man has entered a pot. Bluff him somewhat more often than you would other players. Don't call as liberally when he bets.

Photo 5: Does neatness count?

--- **Photo 6** ---

Title: Building code violations.

Category: Noncombat.

Description: This player isn't terribly concerned about how his chips appear. They are unarranged and uncountable.

Motivation: The player feels like gambling, is poised for action and is not thinking about real money.

Reliability:		
	Weak players =	79%
	Average players =	62%
	Strong players =	53%

Value Per Hour:		
	$1 limit =	$0.27
	$10 limit =	$0.90
	$100 limit =	$2.70

Discussion: Although players will sometimes fool you, haphazardly stacked chips usually mean careless play. This player's game will probably be too liberal, but he might also get good value from his big hands by playing aggressively. There's a good chance this man is prepared to lose all those chips, and often he will.

Best Strategy: Call more often when he bets. Bluff him less frequently than other players.

Caro's Law of Tells #1

Players often stack chips in a manner directly indicative of their style of play. Conservative means conservative; sloppy means sloppy.

Photo by Raiko Hartman

Photo 6: This man doesn't seem to care how many chips he has.

Photo 7

Title: Help, hurry, I want to gamble!

Category: Noncombat.

Description: The man at left is out of chips and he wants more. He's making sure he gets immediate attention by waving his money in the air.

Motivation: This guy doesn't mind letting people know that, at least temporarily, he has money to gamble with. Often he's compensating for the "humiliation" of having lost his chips by making certain everyone knows he isn't broke. He may even feel playful in anticipation of gambling more freely than before. It's rare for a conservative player to use a flamboyant method of buying chips to fool you; that is unusual among weak or average players.

Reliability:

Weak players	= 75%
Average players	= 72%
Strong players	= 55%

Value Per Hour:

$1 limit	= $0.24
$10 limit	= $0.75
$100 limit	= $2.40

Discussion: Even though this tell isn't always accurate, when a man asks for chips in a flamboyant manner, there's a much better than even chance that he's going to play aggressively and often carelessly.

Best Strategy: Until you know differently, treat this man as you would any other loose player. Call more often; bluff less often.

Photo by Raiko Hartman

Photo 7: This man is asking for chips and wants it to be known.

--------------------------------- **Photo 8** ---------------------------------

Title: Where is that $100 I hid here in 1976?

Category: Noncombat.

Description: This man is buying chips, but doesn't want anyone to see what's in his wallet.

Motivation: He is by nature conservative about money. It's possible that he doesn't have much money in his wallet and is embarrassed to show it. Maybe he has a lot of money in his wallet and doesn't want anyone to see it. The general truth is that he simply isn't a flashy player.

Reliability:
Weak players	= 80%
Average players	= 65%
Strong players	= 60%

Value Per Hour:
$1 limit	= $0.15
$10 limit	= $0.33
$100 limit	= $0.90

Discussion: This is exactly the opposite of the previous tell. When you see a player hiding his bankroll, there's a very good chance he'll play conservatively. Usually he won't even lift his wallet above the table to buy chips. He'll guard it in his lap.

Best Strategy: Call him less; bluff him more.

Caro's Law of Tells #2

Players often buy chips in a manner directly indicative of their style of play. Flamboyant means flamboyant; guarded means guarded.

Photo by Lee McDonald

Photo 8: The man is squeezing money from his wallet to buy chips.

Photo 9

Title: I'll bet I can wait longer than you can.

Category: Noncombat.

Description: From the expression on this player's face, his mind seems to be on something other than poker. He's leaning back slumped with his arms folded.

Motivation: This player is not in a gambling mood and is simply relaxing while waiting patiently for a good poker hand.

Reliability:		
Weak players	=	90%
Average players	=	85%
Strong players	=	78%

Value Per Hour:		
$1 limit	=	$0.30
$10 limit	=	$0.54
$100 limit	=	$1.32

Discussion: This sort of body language seems to convey patience and that's exactly right. Here you see that this player has just received his fourth card in seven stud. He apparently has little interest in this pot. It's possible he got the fourth card for free because nobody bet on third street. In any case, this pot isn't very important to him. Players who are winning and wish to sit on their lead will often simply lean back and wait for the good opportunities. True, players often *act* uninterested when they have strong hands, but that isn't the case here. If this man were trying to deceive you, he'd probably do more than just lean back and stare. He'd likely look *away* from the action or even start to throw his hand away prematurely. Those tells will be analyzed later. Take a good look at this man. When you see someone whose mannerisms are similar, you can be pretty sure he'll play only quality hands.

Best Strategy: Seldom get involved in a pot with this man.

Photo by Frank Mitrani

Photo 9: This player is leaning back with his arms folded, relaxing.

Photo 10

Title: I've got better things to do than play poker.

Category: Noncombat.

Description: Again we see a player leaning back and looking uninterested. This time he is not folding his arms.

Motivation: He is feeling patient.

Reliability:

Weak players	= 88%
Average players	= 78%
Strong players	= 68%

Value Per Hour:

$1 limit	= $0.24
$10 limit	= $0.51
$100 limit	= $1.05

Discussion: This is similar to the previous tell. However, when a player has his arms folded, he's generally in a long-range waiting mode. Some players lean slightly forward when they're interested in a hand and otherwise (as in this photo) slump backward. Players may even be aware that they're doing this, but it's too much effort for them to try to camouflage their behavior—especially when they figure nobody is watching for it.

Best Strategy: If you act before this player, play some slightly weaker hands which you would normally pass. That's because this player is no threat to you at the moment. He's making it easier for you to steal the antes.

Photo by Frank Mitrani

Photo 10: This player is also leaning back and appears to be patient.

Photo 11

Title: When will I ever get a chance to stack these chips?

Category: Noncombat.

Description: There are a great deal of chips scattered in front of the woman. That's not because she isn't organized. It's because she just won a giant pot and hasn't had time to stack it.

Motivation: Won last pot.

Reliability:

Weak players	= 85%
Average players	= 80%
Strong players	= 74%

Value Per Hour:

$1 limit	= $0.12
$10 limit	= $0.27
$100 limit	= $0.63

Discussion: Most players like to stack their chips before they get involved in another pot. This doesn't mean they won't play strong hands. A player may even toss in a few chips on medium-strength hands as a courtesy while sorting through the last pot. However, there's one thing players will almost never do in this situation, and that's run a bluff from scratch. True, they may *end up* bluffing, but when they enter pots, it's almost always because their hands merit it.

Best Strategy: If this woman plays a hand while she's still stacking a giant pot, give her credit for having at least medium power. Don't invest money on the hope that she entered the pot bluffing.

Photo by Raiko Hartman

Photo 11: The woman has just won a major pot and the next hand is beginning.

Chapter 2

Sharing A Hand

Once in a while a player will show his hand to someone who isn't involved in the pot. The kibitzer can be a fellow player who has already thrown away his hand. Maybe it's a friend or relative who's just approached the table. Sometimes friends sit nearby to watch their favorite poker hero compete.

You'll find fantastic clues to the strength of an opponent's hand when two players are sharing it. If the onlooker has approached while the hand is already in progress, then *he's* the one to watch. He likely will use subtle kindergarten psychology in an attempt to help the poker-playing friend along. For instance, if the kibitzer has arrived in the middle of the hand, he may sigh sadly if what he sees is very strong. If that hand is weak, he may just keep staring at it admiringly. In this sense, the kibitzer will usually *act* in a manner opposite the strength of the hand he's viewing. Acting strong when weak or weak when strong contributes to many of the tells you'll learn in *Part Two—Tells From Actors*.

But when a hand is shared *from the very beginning,* players tend to follow a trend without knowing it. Then they are not actors; they are unaware. Here is the tell I have in mind...

Photo 12

Title: Let's win this one together, darlin'.

Category: Sharing A Hand.

Description: The man at center is competing for this pot. Sometime *after* he became involved, his girlfriend walked up. At that point he decided it was all right to let her see his cards.

Motivation: Perhaps he wants her to know he's playing a legitimate hand and is not gambling recklessly. He may also want to impress her with his card-playing ability, feeling pretty confident that his hand is good enough to claim the pot.

Reliability: Weak players = 68%
               Average players = 65%
                Strong players = 55%

Value Per Hour: $1 limit = $0.21
                  $10 limit = $0.60
                 $100 limit = $0.66

Discussion: Usually if a man is involved in a hand that he knows he shouldn't be playing, he will *not* share it with a pal, wife or girlfriend who happens along in the midst of poker combat. If he does share it, it's probable that the hand is strong enough to merit his investment. If this guy held poor cards or was bluffing, he would likely be afraid to show his hand for two reasons. First, he might unwillingly impress upon the onlooker that he plays poorly. Second, the onlooker might accidentally tip off to his opponents that his hand is weak, costing him the pot. Strong players are less likely to exhibit this tell, and some may even use it as a ploy to attempt a bluff. Against a strong opponent, watch the onlooker for clues.

Best Strategy: Don't bet into this player or call him with anything less than a solid hand.

Caro's Law of Tells #3

Any unsophisticated player who bets,
then shares his hand while awaiting a call,
is unlikely to be bluffing.

Photo by Raiko Hartman

Photo 12: The man at center is letting the woman share his hand.

Chapter 3

Shuffling A Hand

There are many ways players show their impatience or their anxiety. Many nervous habits can be detected, and rarely is your opponent aware that he's exhibiting these mannerisms.

We'll talk more about this in Chapter 4, titled *Nervousness*. First, be aware that—particularly in draw poker and occasionally in seven stud—players will shuffle their cards before looking at them. Let's see how it works and what it means...

———————————————— **Photos 13 & 14** ————————————————

Title: Don't make me look until I have to.

Category: Shuffling A Hand.

Description: What you see here happens frequently in five card draw poker. Imagine that the woman has drawn one card to a flush. She will continue to take the top card from her hand and place it on the bottom. She'll do this over and over until the action reaches her and it's time to look.

Motivation: She needs to improve her hand to win and doesn't want to see how it comes out just yet. Building suspense is a common habit with some players; it usually happens when they figure they don't have the best hand and must therefore get lucky on the draw.

Reliability:		
Weak players	=	79%
Average players	=	75%
Strong players	=	70%

Value Per Hour:		
$1 limit	=	$0.42
$10 limit	=	$1.50
$100 limit	=	$3.75

Discussion: When you see a player shuffling through his or her cards (usually in draw poker), you should figure the hand requires help. Also, it turns out that there's a much better than average chance that the player is drawing to an especially powerful hand. In draw lowball, many players shuffle only if they're drawing to a bicycle (5-4-3-2-A, the best possible hand) or a six. Players seldom shuffle on less suspenseful lowball draws, such as one-card to a nine. In high-hand-wins draw poker, there's a very great chance that any player prolonging the suspense by shuffling his cards is drawing to a straight or a flush (or even a straight flush). Sometimes you'll find seven-stud players shuffling their three hole cards before looking at their seventh (final) card. As you'd expect, among weak players, this generally means they must improve their hand to win.

Best Strategy: Use logic. Suppose you're playing jacks-or-better-to-open draw poker. You open with a pair of aces. An opponent calls. You draw three; he draws one. You look at your hand and see three aces. Normally you'd be tempted to bet in this situation, because if your opponent was drawing to two pair and it didn't help (which is likely to happen 11 out of 12 times), he'd probably call you anyway. However, when that opponent is shuffling, you should figure that there's a very good chance he's drawing to a straight or a flush, and you should therefore check rather than bet. If the game is lowball and an opponent draws one, shuffles, then bets, you should *not* raise with a smooth seven (such as 7-4-3-2-A), even though you might have raised had he not shuffled.

Photo 13: The woman is shuffling her cards before she looks. She slides the top card off...

Photo 14: ...and puts it on the bottom, then repeats the process.

Chapter 4

Nervousness

Genuine nervousness is hard to fake. Usually you should interpret it for what it means. Fine, but what does it mean? If a poker player seems nervous, is it because he has a strong hand or because he's bluffing?

Many people suspect that players show more nervousness when they're bluffing. After all, there's a great deal of strain involved when you're bluffing and you know everyone's attention is focused on you. Some players are so scared when they bluff that they scarcely breathe.

So, are players with weak hands more likely to show nervousness than players with strong hands? Usually not! And especially not in limit poker. In no-limit games where the strain of bluffing into a large pot can bring genuine nervousness to the surface, you could argue that players are more likely to remain calm when they have a big hand than when they're bluffing.

Not true. Even in no-limit poker, there's an overwhelming tendency for players to *appear* calm when they're bluffing. In a sense, it's an act, so maybe we should include this discussion in *Part Two—Tells From Actors*. But disguising nervousness by conveying calm is not always a conscious act. Often it's something a player who's bluffing does instinctively out of fear of being discovered.

Misinterpreting nervousness can be an extremely expensive poker mistake. That's why I want you to profit by understanding what makes a player shake, what makes him jittery and what makes him impatient.

When a player makes a very big hand, he may begin to shake noticeably. In general, this is a *release of tension* and should not be interpreted as concern over his fate. Many millions of dollars (and that's no exaggeration) are lost every year by calling players who suddenly begin to tremble.

Here's something even more important. If a player has a big hand, has already bet and is waiting for your call, he may tap his finger rhythmically on the table. He is usually unaware he's performing this impatient act. Among many players, even some world-class players, you'll see this (usually in a limit game) only when they are already pretty certain of winning the pot and the only remaining suspense is whether or not you'll call. If this is their habit and once in a while they bet but do *not* tap a finger, you can be almost 100% sure they're either bluffing or they feel the hand is vulnerable.

Remember, most players show obvious outward nervousness *only* when they're in very little danger. If they're in great jeopardy, they struggle to control their nervousness until their fate is decided. Yes, they're nervous, but they won't let you know it if they can help it. One nervous clue to bluffing is very shallow breathing or even the holding of breath.

Additionally, players may be afraid to look at you *or* the pot. On the other hand, they may have read somewhere that players who won't look you in the eye are apt to be bluffing, so they'll compensate by staring at you blatantly. Make sure your opponent isn't trying to fool you, lest you make an erroneous conclusion about his behavior. If you're bound and determined to interpret eye contact, then the most common sign that an opponent is bluffing is if he'll look at you very briefly, offer a semi-smile and then glance away quickly. That's an attempt to look you in the eye and act unafraid. But the action is cut short because the player can't maintain the act under great pressure. In that case, call.

Keep in mind that players who are bluffing genuinely bolster themselves and keep their movements reserved (except for any conscious acts they may try to convey). This means if a player has bet and his knee is jittering beneath the table (you can usually see, feel or sense this), then it is extremely unlikely that he's bluffing. If he normally jerks his knee up and down between and during hands, expect him to *stop* if ever he bluffs. This is a very important tell. Its *Value Per Hour* is much greater than most unaware tells, more than $3 in a typical $10 limit game.

There are other signs of nervousness and impatience that can't be seen. These are discussed under *Part Four—The Sounds of Tells*.

Let's look at two tells dealing with nervousness. . .

───────────── **Photos 15, 16 & 17** ─────────────

Title: It's exciting to come out fighting!

Category: Nervousness.

Description: In Photo 15, the player looks at his final seven stud card. On the board he has three of clubs, eight of hearts, five of spades and six of hearts. You're probably wondering what his first two hole cards were, so I'll tell you: five of hearts, four of hearts. This means that as he looks at his river card (seventh card), he has a pair of fives, a possible straight, a possible flush *and* a possible straight flush. In Photo 16 the magnitude of what he's caught is registering in his mind as he begins to tremble. You can tell, because his right hand is slightly blurry. By the time he completes his bet (Photo 17) his right hand is really shaking. You guessed it, he made the straight flush! Also notice that his left hand continues to grip the river card. He's not looking at it anymore. He's merely pinching it hard in an effort to keep his left hand from shaking also. That's somewhat unusual. Often, a player in this situation would put the river card face down on the table and guard it.

Motivation: Made hand. No control.

Reliability:
                Weak players = 99%
              Average players = 95%
              Strong players = 92%

Value Per Hour:
                  $1 limit = $1.50
                  $10 limit = $5.20
              $100 limit = $49.50

Discussion: The shaking is uncontrollable. Remember, it's a *release of tension,* not fear, that makes this player shake as he bets.

Best Strategy: Pass, unless you also hold something thrilling.

┌───┐
Caro's Law of Tells #4
A trembling bet is a force to be feared.
└───┘

Photo by Frank Mitrani

Photo 15: This player is looking at his final card in seven stud.

Photo by Frank Mitrani

Photo 16: He reaches for chips, beginning to tremble slightly.

Photo by Frank Mitrani

Photo 17: Now he's shaking badly while making his bet.

Photo 18

Title: I can't believe I'm betting! Where can I hide?

Category: Nervousness.

Description: There are two things you should notice here. The bettor (left) is covering his mouth with his hand. That's the tell we're about to examine. But you should also observe that the player at right is reaching for his chips and staring at the bettor. This latter tell will be discussed in *Part Two—Tells From Actors.*

Motivation: There's a reasonable chance that the bettor is covering his mouth to make close scrutiny of his face difficult. He's unaware that he's doing it, though. The reason he unconsciously wants to avoid examination is that he's probably bluffing.

Reliability:

Weak players	= 71%
Average players	= 62%
Strong players	= 57%

Value Per Hour:

$1 limit	= $0.27
$10 limit	= $0.54
$100 limit	= $1.35

Discussion: Those of you familiar with kinesics and "body language" may have already figured out why the bettor is probably bluffing. Many people who put their hands on or near their mouths are not telling the whole truth. Some people have developed this habit for self-conscious reasons even when telling the gospel truth, so this tell isn't 100% accurate, only a fairly good indicator. A 1980 study of lowball players that I conducted in Gardena, California showed only moderate evidence in support of this tell. The scope of the study was 67 clear hand-near-mouth instances. In 44 cases, the bettor was called, but won the pot only 12 times. Three times the bettor was raised and threw his hand away. Although that would seem to indicate that this tidbit can be used pretty effectively at the poker table, be cautious. First, of 32 times that the bettor lost to the caller, we cannot assume that he (or she, as it sometimes happened) was always bluffing. On a few occasions, he may have thrown away a legitimate betting hand upon seeing a stronger hand shown by the caller. Second, it's mathematically possible that the bettor was *never* bluffing on the 20 occasions that he wasn't called. Such a circumstance would dramatically alter the results of the study. In fact,

I specifically noted one case where the bettor wasn't called and showed down a six-four, the second best possible hand, just because he was proud of it. Even considering those words of caution, hand-near-mouth players appeared to be either bluffing or holding weak hands most of the time. This is one of those popular body language behaviorisms which has been well publicized. Its poker value seems to be only marginal. Nevertheless, it's probable that players who position their hands near their mouths are more likely to be bluffing than those who don't.

Best Strategy: When in doubt, call with marginal hands and even weak hands.

Caro's Law of Tells #5

In the absence of indications to the contrary, call any bettor whose hand covers his mouth.

Photo by Allen Photographers

Photo 18: The man at left is betting. Where is his left hand?

Chapter 5

Double-Checking

Players double-check their hands for various reasons. If they've already bet and, under the threat of a call, they look back and *continue to stare* at the hand, there's a very high probability that they are weak or bluffing. That's an *act* designed to make you think they're studying a powerful hand. We'll handle that related subject in *Part Two— Tells From Actors.* It's also discussed in *Part Three—Some General Tells,* in Chapter 22, titled *Gaining Information.* Right now we're dealing with something entirely different.

This section is about genuine instinctive double-checking. You can distinguish it from the *acted* double-check, because in the genuine kind the player will look only long enough to determine whatever he must. Then he'll usually look away and guard his hand. But in cases where that genuine second look finds a bad hand, the player might decide to keep staring at it (for reasons relating to acting). Whether or not the original motive for the double-check was genuine, if the player continues to stare he then holds a weak hand.

If he peeks quickly, then glances away, you must ask yourself: *What could this opponent be checking for?* Usually the answer is apparent. If it's seven stud through fifth street (the fifth card has been dealt) and all three exposed cards are suited, then a quick glance to his hole cards probably means the player is checking to see if he has one more card of that suit. That tell is important because you know immediately that he does not have *two* cards of that suit, so he doesn't yet have a flush. Had he held two suited cards, he'd know it immediately, since the fifth card would have given him the flush he was hoping for. If a player hits a third suited card, then looks quickly at his hole cards, you must reason he does not have a flush and you can confidently bet hands you would otherwise have checked.

Suppose you're playing draw lowball and, after a rash of raises, your opponent draws one card. Suppose, further, that he is guarding the four cards that he's keeping in one hand. With the other hand he reaches for the card he's just drawn and peeks at it. Then he immediately turns his attention to his other cards, double-checking briefly. This should tell you that he caught a *low* card and either made the strong hand or paired. You should, therefore, revise your normal strategy by not betting anything but a premium hand. You should definitely not bet a smooth eight (like 8-5-3-2-A), because your opponent either made a much better hand and will raise, or he paired and will not call. So, you must check. If he subsequently bets, you should call with your eight *only* if you would also call with a king. That's because your eight can win only if he paired and is bluffing. If an eight wins, a king would win also.

Remember, players double-check for a reason. It's your job to figure out what that reason is. Here are some pictures...

─────────── Photos 19 & 20 ───────────

Title: What was my *other* card?

Category: Double-check.

Description: In Photo 19, the man wearing the suit took the initiative by betting. This is seven stud and his exposed card was a king. His opponent's card was a jack. In Photo 20, the man catches an eight off-suit to go with his king. Immediately (and only *briefly,* though not proven by the photo) he looks back at his hole cards.

Motivation: He simply wants to check his hole cards to see if the eight helped him.

Reliability:
Weak players = 70%
Average players = 65%
Strong players = 52%

Value Per Hour:
$1 limit = $0.15
$10 limit = $1.20
$100 limit = $1.50

Discussion: When this player catches the small card and double-checks, you can be pretty sure he has some other small card in the hole. That small card did not have relevance until now. Why? Probably because he had a pair of kings to begin with and some secondary card that was not worth remembering. Catching the eight made him check to see if he caught two pair. If both his face-up cards were suited, a motive for a double-check could be to see if he has one more of that suit in the hole.

Best Strategy: In selecting your strategy, figure that there's a better than average chance that this opponent has a pair of kings and a fair chance he has kings-up. There is almost no chance he has either three kings or three eights. And it's very unlikely that he has a high kicker to go with a pair of kings. Keep these factors in mind, consider your own hand and play accordingly.

Photo by Frank Mitrani

Photo 19: It's seven stud and the man at center is betting on third street. His face-up card is a king. His opponent's card is a jack.

Photo by Frank Mitrani

Photo 20: Now we advance to fourth street. The player at center catches an eight to go with his king, and now he double-checks his hole cards.

Photos 21 & 22

Title: One of my cards was red?

Category: Double-check.

Description: In Photo 21, the player watches the flop. In Photo 22, he realizes that all three flop cards are diamonds and he begins to double-check his hold 'em hand.

Motivation: He wants to find out if he has a diamond.

Reliability: Weak players = 90%
        Average players = 85%
        Strong players = 75%

Value Per Hour: $1 limit = $0.42
        $10 limit = $3.00
      $100 limit = $13.50

Discussion: Players remember denominations (such as king, seven, deuce) more readily than they do suits. Only if both hole cards are suited are unsophisticated hold 'em players apt to be certain of their *exact* cards before the flop. For this reason, if the flop is suited, players must look back to see if they have a card of that suit. When you see a player peek again at his hand, it should tell you that he does not already have a complete flush. However, he may have one card of the suit flopped. His double-check should also let you know that he doesn't have two pair or trips because then he'd know it and he wouldn't need to look. This latter conclusion is a bit dangerous with some players, since they may hold hands like king-seven of clubs, see the flop come king-queen-seven of diamonds and need to check to see if the seven *also* paired them (they can usually remember that the king paired them). In any case, this tell lets us know almost for sure that our opponent doesn't have a flush. This is one reason why you should be watching your opponents when the flop is spread. You can always look at the board later; it won't change.

Best Strategy: If you hold king-jack (top pair with second best possible kicker) and you would bet if the flop weren't suited, you should consider betting anyway against this opponent. If you hold king-queen (two big pair) in no limit and this opponent subsequently moves all in against you, you should be more willing to call than you usually would. That's because there's a good chance he holds something other than a flush.

Perhaps his hand is queen of clubs with ace of diamonds, giving him a draw to the best possible flush *and* a quality pair. Your exact decision in a no limit game would be based on many other factors. Remember, any weak-to-average player who double-checks after the flop is giving you important information to weigh while making your decision.

Photo by Frank Mitrani

Photo 21: The player is watching the dealer spread the flop in hold 'em.

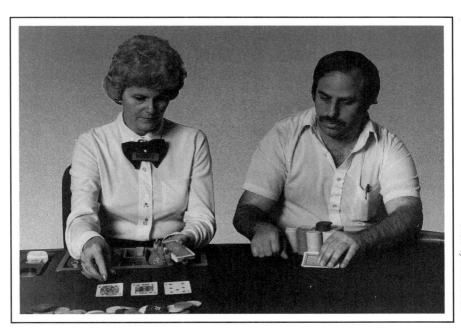

Photo by Frank Mirani

Photo 22: The flop is three diamonds. As soon as he sees it, the player begins to look back at his hand.

Chapter 6

Fearlessness

If I tell you that players who hold cinch winners are unafraid, you'll say: *So what? Everyone in the world knows that.*

True. But not everyone knows how players act at the poker table when they're unafraid. For one thing, players who are fearless are more apt to engage in natural conversation. If someone's holding a royal flush, you can ask him to comment on the politics of the day and he'll be able to talk in a relaxed, rational manner. Had he been bluffing, he'd be apt to either remain silent or force some hazy conversation. What he'd say would be less rational than usual. Don't believe me? Try asking players questions after they've bet into big pots. The ones with the dynamite hands will talk freely; the ones with the vulnerable hands will either remain silent, force their speech or talk jibberish.

What else can I tell you about fearless players who are holding winning hands? Well, it turns out that they sometimes smile broadly. Hey, you've hung around this world for a number of years. You know as well as I do how to tell the difference between a forced smile and a broad genuine smile. When you see a genuine smile, figure the player is happy about his hand. When you see a player force a smile after betting, there's a good chance he's bluffing.

Similarly, any player who has a giggling fit is almost certainly not bluffing (except in a very small game where his fate doesn't matter to him). A genuine giggle is hard to fake. Also, players have no motive to fake a giggle because, strangely enough, giggles don't make their opponents pass; giggles bring attention and make opponents suspicious.

Remember what we talked about in Chapter 4 on *Nervousness*. People who bet and continue to move about impatiently are apt to have big hands. Players who are bluffing don't want to do anything that might trigger your call. Many bluffers feel instinctively that they must remain almost unmoving for fear of giving their hand away and getting called. That's why when you see a very animated player who has bet, you should figure he has a good hand. There is an exception: Some players will use motions and comments specifically designed to make you throw your hand away. When players *act* like they hold big hands, they deserve your call because they're usually weak. But when they're just being themselves, making movements and not trying to restrain themselves, it's unlikely that they're bluffing or even worried.

There is one peculiar habit displayed by some players who are unafraid. These are usually friendly players who after betting may make some gruff remark. Maybe you came right out and asked if he was bluffing and he replied, "Just play the game." You thought this kind of unfriendly remark was out of character for him. What should you do? Probably pass. Players who are bluffing are generally afraid to engage in hostilities. They don't want to make you call out of anger. Ask a bluffer if he's bluffing and you're more apt to hear him chirp something like, "Let me check and see," coupled with a forced smile, or simply "Yes," said in a deliberately unconvincing manner.

Caro's Law of Tells #6

*A genuine smile usually means a genuine hand;
a forced smile is a bluff.*

Caro's Law of Tells #7

*The friendlier a bettor is,
the more apt he is to be bluffing.*

Considering Laws #6 and #7, keep in mind that most players can smile genuinely only when they're feeling fearless. And players are without fear because they hold probable winning hands. The reason bluffers are apt to be friendly is that they are afraid to seem intimidating. They are acting nice so you won't call. Conversely, some players may try to intimidate you into calling when they have winning hands by acting gruffer than their usual manner.

Got it? Great! Now here's a photographic tell that deals with cigarettes...

─────────────── **Photos 23 & 24** ───────────────

Title: Victory and the taste of tobacco.

Category: Fearlessness.

Description: After placing his bet, the man in the suit grasps his cigarette and takes a big puff (Photo 23). In Photo 24 we see him awaiting the call and exhaling noticeably.

Motivation: No fears. Impatience.

Reliability:		
Weak players	=	60%
Average players	=	60%
Strong players	=	60%

Value Per Hour:		
$1 limit	=	$0.15
$10 limit	=	$1.20
$100 limit	=	$7.50

Discussion: Players who are bluffing and are therefore afraid will be reluctant to exhale their cigarette smoke in a conspicuous manner. Remember, bluffers try to do nothing to bring attention to themselves and promote a call. Most bluffers would like to be invisible if they could. When a player exhales a huge cloud of smoke, he's not as likely to be afraid of your call. This is an "unaware" tell that's just about equally valid for strong players as for weak players. It will occur more times per hour, however, in smaller games. Since this tell is only 60% reliable, keep in mind that the opposite of what you expect will frequently happen. Occasionally you'll see a cloud of smoke accompany a bluff, even though your clue should weigh in the opposite direction.

Best Strategy: When you are in doubt, pass.

Photo by Raiko Hartman

Photo 23: The man in the suit has made his bet and now he takes a drag from his cigarette.

Photo by Raiko Hartman

Photo 24: He exhales a big cloud of cigarette smoke.

Chapter 7

Glancing At Chips

This is the most valuable clue you're likely to uncover among those who are unaware of their behavior.

Take beginning players, for instance; they do it. Even average players do it. You'll see this tell when you're watching players with years and years of poker experience. But that's not the best part. World-class pros exhibit this tell! What more could you ask for? Well, there *is* more. Many *world champions* provide you with this tell regularly (or at least they used to until this book came out).

The principle is simple, so let's make it a Law. . .

Caro's Law of Tells #8

A player glances secretly at his chips only when he's considering a bet—and almost always because he's helped his hand.

You must determine, first, that the glance is not an act. If players stare for a long time at their chips *while they think you're watching* that's probably an act—but you won't see it happen often. Usually, they'll look at their hand (or the flop or the stud card they just caught), then immediately to their chips for a brief moment, then away. That's practically never an act because they don't figure you're watching them right then.

Michael Wiesenberg, noted poker and computer authority, contributes a related tell. Players may glance at *your* chips when they intend to bet. This is much less common than glancing at their own chips. Often it means the same thing (that the player likes his hand and is preparing to wager), especially if the glance is immediate and fleeting. However, be advised that, if your opponent looks at your chips long after he realizes what his cards are, he might be measuring whether he can get away with a bluff. He needs to know what your stack looks like before assessing his bluffing possibilities. For that reason, it's more difficult to interpret the tell when your opponent looks at your chips instead of his own. Also, keep in mind that in no-limit games, players may ostentatiously stare at your chips before bluffing. In order for the glance at *your* chips to reliably mean that the player has a good hand and intends to bet, that glance *must be* brief and the player must be *unaware* that you're watching.

For the most part, expect the player to glance at his own chips. We shall dwell on this a little longer, because it's so important.

If you want to use this tell, you must follow this advice:

(1) When the cards are dealt, don't look at them; watch your opponent!

(2) When the flop lands in hold 'em, don't look at it; watch your opponent!

(3) When the next card arrives in stud, don't look at it; watch your opponent!

It's time for some pictures. . .

——————— Photos 25, 26 & 27 ———————

Title: Love card, lots of chips, look yonder.

Category: Glancing At Chips.

Description: Here is a good example of a very important tell. In some games, average players could be big winners if they did nothing but look for this tell and play their normal game. First, the player sees his new seven stud card. Good catch! At this moment his mind tingles gleefully. Automatically, his eyes fall to his chips. Sometimes he may lower his head briefly, which makes detection easier. That's what's happening here. More often, his head will move only slightly and his *eyes* will find his chips. In that case, you must look more closely. In the last photo, the player is looking away and pretending to be unimpressed by his last card. This is a *Weak Means Strong* indication which will be covered in *Part Two—Tells From Actors*.

Motivation: The glance at the chips is instinctive.

Reliability:

Weak players	= 98%
Average players	= 96%
Strong players	= 90%

Value Per Hour:

$1 limit	= $2.60
$10 limit	= $8.00
$100 limit	= $41.00

Discussion: Players will glance only quickly at their chips, then away. You must be looking at the exact moment it happens. It is a very big mistake not to be watching your seven stud opponents when the new cards arrive. You can always look at your own card later. A quick glance at their chips means they helped the hand.

Best Strategy: Look for sandbagging (checking and then raising) opportunities. Sandbagging can be a powerful poker weapon, but it's even more desirable if you know almost for sure that your opponent will bet, as you do in this tell. If you don't have a strong hand, don't hope to catch this man bluffing. He won't be. And, certainly, don't try to bluff him.

Photo by Frank Mitrani

Photo 25: It's seven stud and an ace is being dealt to the man at center.

Photo by Frank Mitrani

Photo 26: He immediately glances down at his chips.

Photo by Frank Mitrani

Photo 27: Now he looks away as if uninterested.

Photos 28, 29 & 30

Title: Great flop. . . better make sure my chips are still here.

Category: Glancing At Chips.

Description: The quick-glance-at-chips tell occurs very frequently in hold 'em. In Photo 28, the flop registers in the player's mind. Instinctively she looks at her chips (Photo 29). But you have to watch closely or you'll miss it, because by Photo 30—less than one second later—she's looking toward the flop.

Motivation: An instinctive reaction after the flop helps her hand.

Reliability:
Weak players = 98%
Average players = 96%
Strong players = 90%

Value Per Hour:
$1 limit = $2.75
$10 limit = $9.50
$100 limit = $40.00

Discussion: This is very similar to—and, in fact, conceptually identical to—the previous tell. This woman does not look away from the action, however. Instead, she pretends to study the flop. Of course, she already knows very well that the flop helped her, so she doesn't need to study. She's just trying to make you think she's weaker than she is. If you were watching the flop—as even most professional players invariably do—you would have missed this very profitable opportunity and you wouldn't know that the woman now holds a strong hand.

Best Strategy: You need a stronger hand than usual to compete. Don't bluff this woman. Don't expect to catch her bluffing. If you have a mind to check and raise, this is a good opportunity.

Photo by Lee McDonald

Photo 28: It's hold 'em and here come the flop.

Continued

Photo by Lee McDonald

Photo 29: Immediately the player (right) looks at her chips.

Photo by Lee McDonald

Photo 30: But the glance is brief and now she is pretending to study the flop.

Chapter 8

Sudden Interest

Always be alert for a player who suddenly perks up and plays a pot. Usually it takes a genuine hand to rouse a player from a lethargic condition and get him interested in gambling. Often a player will be daydreaming or leaning back, content to wait for the good hands (usually because he's winning). Look! Suddenly, he leans forward and adjusts his posture. He may merely squirm on his chair until he's sitting slightly straighter. This kind of mannerism means the player has a decent hand and is preparing to play.

Also, if he's humming or whistling (handled under *Part Four—The Sounds of Tells*) and then mysteriously stops, it's very likely he holds a hand that pleases him. Normally players who are involved in conversation and then fall silent or lose their ability to form meaningful sentences are about to play a hand.

Those are some signs of sudden interest.

Look at Photo 9 in Chapter 1, *Noncombat Tells*. That man is leaning back, relaxing. He is not likely to play the next pot. Contrast that posture to the following...

─────────────── **Photo 31** ───────────────

Title: This hand might be worth the bother.

Category: Sudden Interest.

Description: This player has been sitting back with his arms folded, watching the world go by. He's winning and doesn't want to risk much of his profit. Suddenly, he receives a jack for his face-up card in seven stud. Extending his arm, and still leaning back, he looks at his hole cards. Then, suddenly, he begins to adjust his posture, shuffling until he is sitting straighter and leaning somewhat forward.

Motivation: He is unconsciously preparing to get involved.

Reliability: Weak players = 77%
Average players = 65%
Strong players = 55%

Value Per Hour: $1 limit = $0.15
$10 limit = $0.33
$100 limit = $0.75

Discussion: It's a mistake to think a player who suddenly adjusts his posture is acting in a manner he hopes will mislead you. Much more frequently, the player is unaware of his action, particularly if he's a novice. You can substantiate this by noting the times when players adjust their postures; you'll discover that it's usually when they are not conscious that you're watching them, making it unlikely that they're acting. Furthermore, the adjustment will usually be brief—also indicating the player isn't trying to draw attention to himself. The exact strength of this seven-stud player's hand depends somewhat on the cards of his opponents, his position relative to the first bettor and how heavy the action is so far. What we do know is that he likes his cards.

Best Strategy: Unless this man holds a strong speculative hand, such as king, queen, jack of the same suit, he probably has at least a pair of jacks. It's likely that he has a buried pair even higher than jacks or even three of a kind. So plan your tactics accordingly, enter the pot with caution and don't try to bluff.

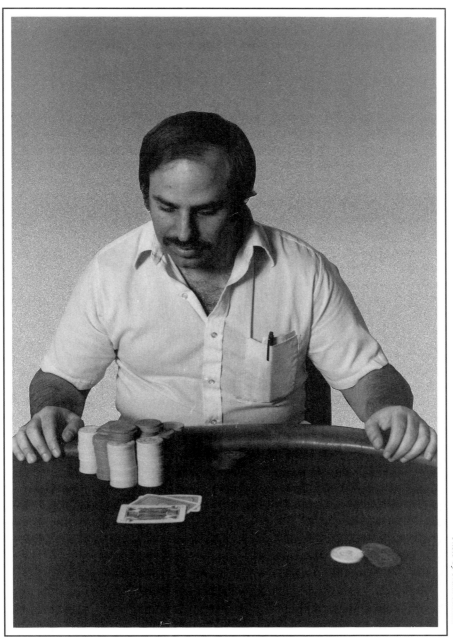

Photo by Frank Mitrani

Photo 31: This man is adjusting his posture and sitting straighter than before.

Chapter 9

Tough Decisions

One strange thing about *limit* poker players—beginners and great ones, too—is that they don't mind letting you know when they have a tough decision.

However, the same is *not* true of no-limit players. In *limit* games, there's a common trait among players who have been bet into and are now faced with a dilemma. They may grumble, discuss the hand aloud, or even sigh and say something like, "Oh, golly, I wish you wouldn't have bet. Now what should I do?" Very often, they'll rock back in their chairs and contemplate.

There's one truth you should always keep in mind. Although players are invariably actors on occasions, they seldom waste a lot of your time and theirs in a limit game if there's no *real* decision involved. Don't expect a player to use thirty seconds to consider a call, then raise. That sort of maneuver is unwelcome in limit games and few players risk their popularity by using it. (Novices sometimes do it, not realizing it's rude.) The reason players don't spend a lot of time *acting* like they're unsure and then raising in limit poker is quite simple. The amount of money at stake relative to the size of the pot is seldom overwhelming. In a no-limit game, there may be a total of $500 already bet and a player now wagers another $500. Here the opponent starts to ponder. There's a good chance that he's putting on an act and will end up raising.

If he decides to add $5000 to the pot, the original bettor might also decide to take a long time before making his decision. That's the way of no-limit poker; hesitation is reasonable.

But, let's say you're playing $20 straight limit (where every bet must be exactly $20). There's $100 in the pot already and now someone bets $20. In response, a player grumbles, leans back and starts to wonder. This is a sign of a genuine dilemma. He's probably considering whether or not to call; raising is not among his options. Remember, the pace in a limit game is much faster than the pace in a no-limit game. Also, decisions in limit games are usually proportionally less important. Keeping those two things in mind, it's easy to see why long hesitation in a limit game usually means a genuine tough decision.

So what should you do if an opponent is showing signs of not knowing whether or not to call?

First, let's examine why a player might be in doubt. Obviously, most rational opponents are in doubt because they don't know if a call is a good investment. In-depth mathematics is not the focus of this book; however, if a pot is $80 large and a call would cost $10, the player must decide if he has at least one chance in nine of winning. If he figures to win more than one such pot out of nine, he's making a good investment—take my word for it. A hesitant player probably feels he has *almost exactly* one chance in nine of winning, even if his evaluation is merely unconscious or intuitive. Your strategy is simple. If you made a legitimate bet with any meaningful hand, you probably want his call. If you're bluffing, you don't.

Remember that, against typical opponents, almost all your physical actions will encourage a call. Players came to the game wanting to put their money in action. If you have the best hand, you should provide your opponent with excuses for making losing calls. Shuffle your cards, talk jibberish, smile insanely, tap the table. All these things bring attention to yourself, make your opponent suspicious, and give him an excuse to call.

So, now you know the following: (1) When an opponent in a limit poker game hesitates for a long time or gives any other indication that he is bothered by your bet, he is probably sincerely uncertain about whether to call; (2) If you've bet with a strong hand, you should be animated and try to coax the opponent into calling; and (3) If you've bet with a weak hand, you should remain fairly still and, thus, encourage your opponent to pass.

It's important to note that most opponents will also remain still when bluffing and be more animated and friendly when holding a big hand. Even though you can use that knowledge against them, don't worry about providing these same tells yourself. It's very unlikely that your opponents are alert enough to read you correctly, so there's more profit to be won by using blatant manipulation than by wearing a poker face.

Now let's look at some genuine indecision . . .

---------------------------- **Photos 32 & 33** ----------------------------

Title: Let me think awhile.

Category: Tough Decisions.

Description: All seven cards have been dealt out in this stud game. The player at left has been doing the betting most of the way. But on the final card, the woman does the betting (Photo 32). At this point the man is faced with a genuine dilemma and must reevaluate his hand. He leans back to think it over (Photo 33).

Motivation: Genuine doubt.

Reliability:

Weak players	= 65%
Average players	= 70%
Strong players	= 70%

Value Per Hour:

$1 limit	= $0.18
$10 limit	= $1.20
$100 limit	= $6.30

Discussion: Players will seldom delay limit poker games by taking an extra-long time to make a decision. When this man leans back and considers his situation, it's probably a genuine borderline choice.

Best Strategy: If you're the bettor faced with this reaction, you should encourage the call if you've made the bet on the strength of your hand. If you're bluffing, discourage the call. It's at times like this—when your opponent is experiencing genuine doubt—that manipulation works best. Also, if your opponent comes out raising after a long hesitation, there's almost a fifty percent chance that he's bluffing, and a call is correct.

Photo by Frank Mirani

Photo 32: The woman is betting her seven-stud hand into the man at left.

Photo by Frank Mitrani

Photo 33: In response, he leans back and ponders.

Chapter 10

Instant Reaction

Before trying a bluff, most players will take time to consider. In limit games, the delay may be only a few seconds, but *there is a delay.* A player needs time to calculate his chances and bolster his courage before bluffing. Additionally, bluffers are afraid to do anything unusual which might encourage your call. Even if it isn't on a conscious level, they know to not bluff too quickly. Experience has taught most players that an instantaneous bet looks suspicious and is not likely to succeed as a bluff.

For this reason, when a player draws three cards, looks at them, then glances *instantly* at his chips and begins to bet without hesitation, you can be pretty sure he has made a hand so obviously strong that it doesn't require consideration.

Conversely, if he checks instantly you can bet that it didn't help. Improvement, when followed by a check, requires evaluation—and evaluation takes time. True, a player might sometimes bet instantly in that smooth chain reaction that goes: look-at-cards, look-at-chips, grab-for-chips. Just remember, that happens only if the hand made is especially strong and no decision is required. Seldom will you see a player make aces-up and bet instantly. That's because betting aces-up in draw poker is usually a borderline decision that requires time for consideration. The same law governs all forms of poker.

Caro's Law of Tells #9

*If a player looks and then checks instantly,
it's unlikely that he improved his hand.*

Caro's Law of Tells #10

*If a player looks and then bets instantly,
it's unlikely that he's bluffing.*

—————————————— **Photos 34 & 35** ——————————

Title: No help, I'll wait.

Category: Instant Reaction.

Description: This is draw poker and the player at center is drawing three to a pair of aces (Photo 34). In Photo 35, he looks and—almost at the same time—pounds his fist on the table to check.

Motivation: No reason to hesitate.

Reliability: Weak players = 94%
                     Average players = 87%
                      Strong players = 60%

Value Per Hour: $1 limit = $0.45
                      $10 limit = $3.00
                     $100 limit = $7.50

Discussion: If this man had made aces-up or three aces, he'd have to evaluate the hand in the light of this new strength. This typically takes a few seconds. When this hesitation is not present, it's clear that the player didn't improve.

Best Strategy: If you have any two pair or a stronger hand, bet. You'll even profit by betting a pair of aces with a king kicker.

Photo 34: The draw poker player (center) is asking for three cards.

Photo 35: He looks and checks almost simultaneously.

—————————— **Photos 36, 37 & 38** ——————————

Title: I probably don't need any help.

Category: Instant Reaction.

Description: It's draw poker, and the man wearing the hat doesn't announce his draw until after the opener (second from left) has declared that he needs three cards (Photo 36). In response, the hatted man draws one in Photo 37. In Photo 38, he looks at the card he's just drawn. This happens *before* the opener announces his bet or check.

Motivation: The one-card draw is not suspenseful enough to delay looking.

Reliability: Weak players = 62%
                    Average players = 58%
                    Strong players = 55%

Value Per Hour: $1 limit = $0.54
                        $10 limit = $2.40
                        $100 limit = $11.70

Discussion: Here is another type of instant reaction. It's draw poker. When the opener takes three cards, the man in the hat realizes that two pair is the probable winner. So, if he has two pair, he knows immediately that he has the better hand before the draw. He tells himself that although he may make a full house, he probably won't *need* to make one. In such a situation, the degree of suspense is less than maximum and the player is likely to look at his card as soon as he receives it. If, however, he is drawing one card to a straight or a flush, he must help his hand in order to win. He is then the underdog. There is a great deal more suspense involved under such circumstances. In suspenseful all-or-nothing situations, many players enjoy not looking until they must. Therefore, when this player looks at his one-card draw instantly, you can figure it's likely that he has two pair, not a straight or a flush attempt. This tell is not nearly 100%, as you can see, but it works very consistently with some players. Among opponents who will sometimes look at their card immediately and sometimes wait, it's overwhelming that they hold two pair (or even three of a kind with a kicker) when they look instantly. This is *not* purely a draw poker tell. In all forms of poker, you can figure that players who won't look until they *must* are likely to need improvement.

Best Strategy: If you are the opener who drew three cards, bet if you make aces-up or queens-up. You're likely to get a call from a smaller two pair—two pair which your opponent almost certainly won't bet for you if you check.

Photo 36: The player second from left is drawing three cards while his opponent at center watches.

Photo by Raiko Hartman

Continued

Photo 37: The man at center draws one. . .

Photo 38: . . .and then he looks at it immediately.

———————— Photos 39, 40, 41 & 42 ————————

Title: You go first.

Category: Instant Reaction (opposite).

Description: This sequence shows the opposite of what happened in the previous sequence. Instead of looking instantly at his one-card draw, the player at center decides to wait and heighten the suspense.

Motivation: He holds a suspenseful hand whose all-or-nothing fate need not be decided yet.

Reliability:		
	Weak players	= 62%
	Average players	= 56%
	Strong players	= 54%

Value Per Hour:		
	$1 limit	= $0.60
	$10 limit	= $2.85
	$100 limit	= $12.00

Discussion: No matter what kind of poker game you're involved in, when you can determine which players need to improve their hand and which players already have a decent hand, you can confidently make bets when you would otherwise have checked, and you can check dangerous hands you might otherwise have bet. See the previous tell (Photos 36, 37 & 38) and remember that players who must improve to win are in more suspenseful situations than those who feel they might already have a winning hand. That's important, because players in suspenseful situations are likely to wait before looking; players in low-pressure situations are apt to look right away.

Best Strategy: Check all medium-strength hands.

Photo 39: The opener (player second from left) draws three.

Photo 40: The man in the hat takes only one.

Photo by Raiko Hartman

Photo 41: The opener watches as the one-card drawer refuses to look until later.

Photo by Raiko Hartman

Photo 42: Now the one-card drawer guards his hand and waits for the opener to act.

Chapter 11

Protecting A Hand

Most players unconsciously guard good cards more carefully than bad cards. While this is more common among weak players, the trait is found at all levels of play and in all forms of poker.

Even the rarely played five card stud provides instances of this tell, because players with good hands tend to show more concern when you reach toward their hole card. Of course, you must not actually touch or even physically approach the opponent's hole card—that's poor poker etiquette. But you can make an ambiguous gesture that your opponent might misinterpret as an invasion of his space. In response, an opponent holding a strong hand will usually jerk unconsciously and assume a more rigid position. He may even fend you off with a stiff arm used as a barrier. Players with weak hands are more lax. They wouldn't care if you reached all the way over and exposed the hole card. Then they could argue that they were entitled to a portion of the pot.

This kind of protective reaction applies to all varieties of poker. However, you don't need to make threatening gestures toward an opponent's cards to utilize this tell. Most opponents will give you clues without any provocation, and this is especially easy to understand if we focus on draw poker.

─────────────── **Photos 43, 44, 45 & 46** ───────────────

Title: I better not let these get away.

Category: Protecting A Hand.

Description: Most draw players look at their cards in a more clandestine manner than what's shown in Photo 43. In small-limit home games and in public casinos where flexible plastic cards are used, the method pictured is sometimes observed. In any case, what's important is whether the player protects his cards *after* he sees them. Two aces and a king on the first three cards is a nice catch, so in Photo 44, the player pushes them securely into his left hand. In Photo 45, the final two cards are viewed: ace and king. That gives this player aces-full. Photo 46 shows him squeezing this treasure very tightly between his fingers.

Motivation: Most people guard important belongings.

Reliability:		
	Weak players	= 90%
	Average players	= 80%
	Strong players	= 70%

Value Per Hour:		
	$1 limit	= $1.10
	$10 limit	= $4.40
	$100 limit	= $16.00

Discussion: Be cautious in using this tell, because some players guard all hands. A few will even use a carefully guarded hand as a ploy to make you think that their weak hand is awesome. That's rare, though, because most players realize that the manner in which a hand is guarded is not something most opponents observe. Knowing this, a player who's weak will not generally go to the trouble of guarding his hand for deception. For that reason, protecting a hand is a topic that fits neatly into this section, *Part One—Tells From Those Who Are Unaware.* The governing truth is that closely protected hands are usually strong. Sometimes, you can even draw a correlation between the amount of protection and the exact strength of the hand. In this photo sequence, the player picks up a full house and makes certain it is secure. There's one other tell at work here, but it belongs in *Part Two—Tells From Actors.* It is this: In the final photo (46), the player is acting almost as if he's about to throw his hand away out of turn. That almost always means he has a good hand, as we'll soon see. Speaking of acting, we'll also soon learn how the typical player might behave if he had been dealt garbage cards instead of a full house. Rather than guard them, he'd be likely to *stare* at them. But that's a topic we must deal with in the pages ahead, as we shift from players who are unaware to actors who are trying to deceive you.

Best Strategy: Assume you're sitting two seats to the right of this player. You wouldn't have seen that he has aces-full, but you'd know he holds something pretty good. You should elect not to open the pot with marginal hands. If this player opens, you should pass with all borderline hands. If you hold an extremely strong hand yourself (say, a straight flush) in jacks-or-better-to-open, you might elect to check rather than open, knowing this player will open for you.

Photo by Frank Mitrani

Photo 43: It's draw poker and, while the deal is in progress, the player looks at his first three cards.

Continued

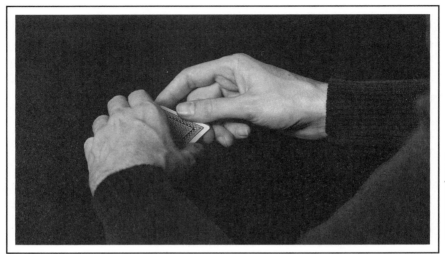

Photo 44: He shelters them in his left hand.

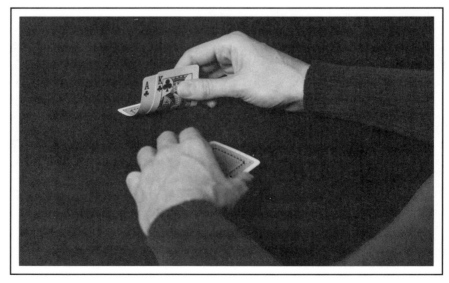

Photo 45: He looks at his next two cards, which complete a full house.

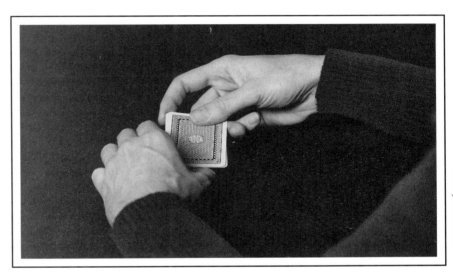

Photo by Frank Mitrani

Photo 46: Immediately, he guards these also.

Part Two

Tells From Actors

In 1977, I contributed these words to Doyle Brunson's classic book *Super/System—A Course In Power Poker*...

> Most people are prevented from living life as they want. In childhood, they're required to do chores they hate. They grow up having to conform at school. As adults they must shake hands they don't want to shake, socialize with people they dislike, pretend they're feeling "fine" when they're feeling miserable, and *act* in control of situations where, in truth, they feel frightened and unsure.
>
> These people—the majority of folks you meet every day—are actors. They present themselves to you as people different than they really are.
>
> Deep within themselves they know they are not the same people they pretend to be. On an unconscious level, they think, "Hey, I'm so phony that if I don't act to disguise my poker hand, everyone will see right through me!"
>
> And that's why the majority of these pitiful people are going to *give* you their money by always acting weak when they're strong and strong when they're weak.

There are six chapters in *Part Two* in addition to the two titled *Weak Means Strong* and *Strong Means Weak*. But don't let that fool you. All of the tells discussed here in *Part Two* are related to those first two chapters. Once you understand the basic concept and apply it, poker domination will become easy and your wallet will begin to bulge.

Before you can use the tells provided by an actor, you must be fairly certain that he's acting and not simply unaware. Determining that truth is not usually difficult. It's probably an act if the player has reason to believe you might be observing a specific mannerism *and* it is of obvious value to him that your conclusion is wrong. I'll say that again, so you don't simply rush past this powerful truth. An opponent is probably acting if: (1) He believes you're watching or listening; and (2) Your decision matters to him.

Since usually both those conditions must be true for a player to act, you may occasionally see beginners start to pass out of turn when they're genuinely not interested in the pot. They may be aware you're watching (the first condition), but your decision doesn't matter (the second condition) because they plan on passing anyway. Such straightforward tells are not usually the case, as we'll soon see. Most players feel an obligation to the game and, in this example, usually won't pass out of turn. Therefore, when they act as if to pass and are aware you're watching, there's a very strong probability that they'll actually bet or raise.

Since a minority of players will not fall into the *weak means strong* and *strong means weak* mode, you should mentally note who they are so you won't err by perpetually applying these tells in those special cases.

Also keep in mind that, overall, strong players are less apt to provide you with tells than weak or average players. Beyond just denying you some of the more common tells, world-class opponents often try to deceive you by reversing some of the more obvious tells. That's right, they may sometimes act weak and *be* weak. You should place such opponents on a "tricky" list in your head and evaluate their behavior carefully.

Fortunately, even poker superstars will provide you with important tells quite regularly. But, for the most part, ordinary players are more predictable and more profitable.

Chapter 12

Weak Means Strong

Poker players like to fool you. If they can convince you that they have a weak hand when they have a strong hand, they figure they'll win a few extra calls and make a few extra dollars.

That reasoning is exactly right. If you let these actors succeed in fooling you, they'll win your money when they hold strong hands. Don't let that happen. The very same acts, which are designed to steal your money, will supply you with powerful information that can place your opponents' bankrolls at your mercy.

When players go out of their way to act weak, it's because they hold strong hands. Remember that. Would you expect a player who truly holds a weak hand to tell you he's in bad shape? That would be stupid. Would you expect a bluffer to tell you he's bluffing? Not me! If they act weak, it can only be because they're strong.

Caro's Law of Tells #11

Disappoint any player who,
by acting weak, is seeking your call.

———————————————— **Photo 47** ————————————

Title: Ah, what's the difference? I bet.

Category: Weak Means Strong.

Description: Here's a seven stud player who's accompanying his bet with a shrug.

Motivation: He wants to make you think he's unsure of his bet.

Reliability:
Weak players = 93%
Average players = 90%
Strong players = 80%

Value Per Hour:
$1 limit = $0.55
$10 limit = $3.20
$100 limit = $11.00

Discussion: Hey, what can I tell you about a shrug that you don't already know? If you ask a friend how he's feeling and you get a polite shrug in response, that's supposed to substitute for, "I'm not really sure. Things could be better." And that's exactly what a poker player is trying to convey when he shrugs and bets. He's suggesting he's not certain about the bet and that his hand could be a lot stronger. Well, don't you believe it! There's only one reason this guy would go out of his way to make you think he has a doubtful betting hand. It's because he holds an almost certain winner.

Best Strategy: Call only with powerful hands; in fact, *just* call with most hands that suggest a raise. Don't try to bluff.

Photo by Raiko Harman

Photo 47: The man at center is shrugging.

Photo 48

Title: Maybe I'll throw this card away, or maybe I'll raise. . .

Category: Weak Means Strong.

Description: It's seven stud and the player at left is betting his ten into his opponent's king. In response, the opponent suggests that he's going to pass by beginning to turn the king face down.

Motivation: The opponent wants to make the bet appear safe.

Reliability:
Weak players = 75%
Average players = 85%
Strong players = 60%

Value Per Hour:
$1 limit = $0.18
$10 limit = $0.83
$100 limit = $1.05

Discussion: Suppose you were in a seven stud game with a king up. There are two other players still to act behind you. You have a king and a queen in the hole, giving you a pair of kings. When the guy with the ten showing starts to bet, does that make you happy or sad? It makes you happy. But, poker players being poker players, you can't be 100% sure that the guy will complete this bet. He probably has a pair of tens at best, so you certainly hope he does complete the bet. What occurs to you, and what occurs to most players, is that it's beneficial to make certain he goes through with the bet. One obvious way of doing this is to start to fold somewhat out of turn. When the bet is made, the player at right will probably act as if he had only been readjusting his card. He'll re-position it and then there's a good chance he'll raise. Except for novices and discourteous opponents, few players pass out of turn when they're weak. That's why if an opponent acts like he's going to pass, you'd better beware.

Best Strategy: If you're the man at left, pass.

Photo by Frank Mitrani

Photo 48: While the seven-stud player bets (left), his opponent begins to turn his *up card* over.

––––––––––––––––––– **Photos 49 & 50** –––––––––––––

Title: Maybe I should stand pat on this full house after all.

Category: Weak Means Strong.

Description: You'll often see inexperienced poker players pretend to draw just before rapping pat. That's exactly what happens in these two photos.

Motivation: An almost instinctive act to confuse the opener.

Reliability: Weak players = 77%
                Average players = 59%
                Strong players = 54%

Value Per Hour: $1 limit = $0.17
                  $10 limit = $0.85
                  $100 limit = $0.90

Discussion: Some players are almost compulsive about disguising their hands. Even if there is little logical benefit in fooling you at the moment, they may still give it a try. When a player who normally doesn't indicate how many he'll draw until it's his turn suddenly decides to let you "know" he needs cards, there's a good chance he'll end up rapping pat. The reason this tell has a fairly low dollar value is because there's very little you can do to capitalize. If you're the opener with a pair of queens, you're going to have to draw three anyway (unless you can split openers and try for a straight or flush). You can gain some ground by knowing that your opponent will probably never rap pat now unless he has a complete hand. He feels that he's made you suspicious and more likely to call by requesting one card out of turn and then changing his mind.

Best Strategy: You're playing draw poker with the joker and have asked for one card. You hold . . .

You should consider throwing away the deuce of diamonds and trying for the flush. Even this has disadvantages, because your opponent may have a pat full house and you'll end up drawing dead. If you've asked for three cards to a pair of kings, there's very little you can do at this point; except that if you make three kings and your opponent raps pat, you should not call when he subsequently bets.

Photo by Frank Mitrani

Photo 49: Here we're playing draw poker. The opener (left) is throwing away three cards while an opponent (second from left) acts as if he's going to discard one.

Photo by Frank Mitrani

Photo 50: But now that the opener has already received his three card draw, his opponent "changes his mind" and raps pat.

——————————————— **Photo 51** ———————————————

Title: Don't worry about me. . .yet!

Category: Weak Means Strong.

Description: The player (second from left) is betting. What's interesting is that his opponent (center) is looking away from the bet.

Motivation: The opponent does not want to discourage or challenge the bettor.

Reliability:	
Weak players	= 98%
Average players	= 92%
Strong players	= 80%

Value Per Hour:	
$1 limit	= $1.85
$10 limit	= $10.30
$100 limit	= $62.00

Discussion: Spend some time reviewing this photo. Always keep in mind that players who look away from the action are more dangerous than those who watch or look at the bettor. The man at center does not want to do anything to discourage the bet. Expect him to raise. This is a very important tell.

Best Strategy: Don't put any more money into this pot unless you have a very strong hand. If you're the bettor, you should probably abandon your wager now!

Photo 51: The man in the middle is the one to watch.

Photos 52, 53 & 54

Title: I try to look bored before I pounce!

Category: Weak Means Strong.

Description: In this sequence, you see that the player in the foreground has picked up a full house, first ace-ace-seven and then ace-seven. That's a terrific hand and, as you'd expect after reading *Part One—Tells From Those Who Are Unaware,* he guards this hand securely. But that's not what we're focusing on here. There's something even more overwhelming happening here. Having secured his aces-full, the player now looks to the left, away from the approaching action.

Motivation: He doesn't want to look like a threat.

Reliability:

Weak players	=	92%
Average players	=	90%
Strong players	=	78%

Value Per Hour:

$1 limit	=	$1.00
$10 limit	=	$5.50
$100 limit	=	$43.00

Discussion: This is similar to the previous tell, except here it's draw poker and the player looks away before the pot is even opened. Coupled with the fact that he guards his hand securely (an *unaware* tell), this is a very predictable situation. The man is acting as if he is uninterested, therefore he's interested. It's that simple.

Best Strategy: If you have an opening hand and must act before this player, you should usually check and let him open. If you have only a medium-strength hand, don't play.

Photo by Raiko Hartman

Photo 52: This sequence begins with the draw poker player in the foreground (you can see part of his face at right) picking up his first three cards.

Photo by Raiko Hartman

Photo 53: Now the next two cards.

Continued

Photo by Raiko Hartman

Photo 54: His whole hand is guarded and he looks away as the action approaches clockwise.

Photos 55 & 56

Title: Don't worry about me...I'm only going to raise!

Category: Weak Means Strong.

Description: In Photo 55 the woman is studying the flop. Few hold 'em players will watch anything but the board when the dealer spreads the flop. It is a key moment of suspense and it's only human that poker players want to see what comes off the deck. Almost immediately she looks away from the flop, the pot and the action (Photo 56).

Motivation: She likes the flop, but doesn't want to appear threatening.

Reliability: Weak players = 96%
Average players = 94%
Strong players = 77%

Value Per Hour: $1 limit = $1.45
$10 limit = $7.25
$100 limit = $38.00

Discussion: This is a tremendous hold 'em tell. As you've learned, players who look away from the action are giving you profitable information in all forms of poker. But when the flop comes in hold 'em, this tell is especially easy to detect.

Best Strategy: Play only very strong hands. If there's a subsequent bet, abandon any hand that you feel would normally be marginal or even slightly profitable. If you have a strong hand, try to let this woman do your betting for you. You dare not bluff.

Photo by Frank Mitrani

Photo 55: It's hold 'em and the woman watches the flop.

Photo by Frank Mitrani

Photo 56: Now she quickly looks away.

Photos 57, 58, 59 & 60

Title: Go ahead and bet your two pair, sucker!

Category: Weak Means Strong.

Description: Focusing on the player in the foreground (not fully shown), we see that he is hoping for a straight in Photo 57. He makes it in Photo 58, protects his hand in Photo 59 and, finally, acts like he's going to throw his three hole cards away in Photo 60.

Motivation: He feels he has the winning hand and wants to make his opponent's bet seem safe.

Reliability:	Weak players	=	73%
	Average players	=	65%
	Strong players	=	55%

Value Per Hour:	$1 limit	=	$0.35
	$10 limit	=	$2.10
	$100 limit	=	$8.50

Discussion: It's the last photo that you should concentrate on now. In any type of poker, players who act like they're going to discard their hands before the action reaches them should be considered a threat. There's no reason for them to use this maneuver unless they're trying to fool you. This is definitely a tell where the player is trying to act weak because he is strong. Here, he has a double motive. Not only is he telling his opponent at left that the bet is safe, he's encouraging the other opponent (who must act next) to call.

Best Strategy: Abandon all bets! Even if you have a very strong hand, it's usually better to let the man with the straight bet for you. You can later raise with your full house. Don't bluff and don't expect to catch the player in the foreground bluffing. Not this time.

Photo 57: In the foreground, someone is picking up his final card in seven stud. A five or a ten would complete a straight.

Photo 58: It's a five.

Continued

Photo by Lee McDonald

Photo 59: The player carefully places the five with his other two hole cards.

Photo 60: While the opponent to his left bets, he acts as if he's going to throw his hand away.

105

-- **Photo 61** --

Title: Don't worry about me, I'm not even watching!

Category: Weak Means Strong.

Description: Look at the man across the table. This is a very common mannerism. While it's true that most beginners and even some medium-level players holding big hands will exaggerate their actions to appear weak, most sophisticated players won't. What you see here is a man acting a little bit weak because he has a strong hand. He's looking away, but only slightly. His mannerism is more subtle than the ones we've been studying.

Motivation: He doesn't want to discourage your bet.

Reliability: Weak players = 80%
                  Average players = 74%
                  Strong players = 78%

Value Per Hour: $1 limit = $0.15
                     $10 limit = $7.25
                     $100 limit = $80.00

Discussion: This tell is not much different than a player holding a full house and staring blatantly away from the table. Look closely and you'll see that the man across the table is looking slightly away as the bet enters the pot. Since he's a sophisticated player, he won't exaggerate this act, but he still applies this universal *Weak Means Strong* trick on a more refined level. He's trying to fool you and he looks ready to pounce...because he *is* ready to pounce.

Best Strategy: Don't bet moderately strong hands in the hope of getting a weak call. He doesn't have a weak hand, so a weak call is impossible! *You* need a big hand to call if he bets. This is not a good opportunity to bluff and you won't *be* bluffed.

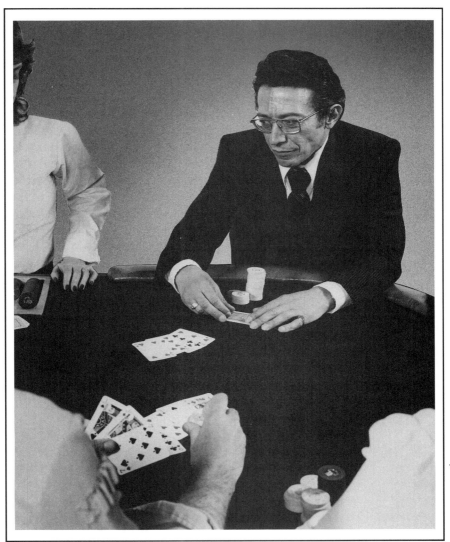

Photo by Lee McDonald

Photo 61: At bottom left, a man is betting. Across the table, the opponent waits without watching.

──────── **Photos 62, 63, 64, 65, 66, 67 & 68** ────────

Title: How long should I wait before I raise?

Category: Weak Means Strong.

Description: In limit poker games, players make their choices promptly. In no-limit games, it's customary to take more time. This is a very important sequence. In Photo 62 the player in the foreground bets, but that's not all! Across the table the opponent makes no movement to prevent the bet. In order to correctly interpret the final strength of the opponent's hand, we must keep this in mind. Even skilled no-limit players will often make some minor gestures to prevent a bet they don't want. They may do this by staring at you, reaching toward their chips or any number of mannerisms to be discussed in the next chapter, *Strong Means Weak*. After the initial bet, the player studies and studies until, in Photo 66, he finally "makes up his mind." Then he moves "all-in" with his chips.

Motivation: The long hesitation is designed to make the original bettor think that the raise is a tough decision.

Reliability:	Weak players	=	80%
	Average players	=	75%
	Strong players	=	65%
Value Per Hour:	small no-limit	=	$ 1.85
	medium no-limit	=	$12.00
	large no-limit	=	$90.00

Discussion: When a no-limit player does nothing to discourage a sizable bet, then hesitates for a long time and chooses to make a large raise, there's little chance that he's bluffing. His long delay is an effort to make you think his raise is marginal and therefore weak. Some professionals may argue that *any* player who makes a large raise is likely to have a very strong hand whether he hesitates long or not. While this may be true, it's also a fact that a player is *even more* likely to have a winning hand if he takes longer than an average amount of time to act. Remember, though, in no-limit poker an *average amount of time* can be half a minute or more, whereas in limit games most decisions require only a few seconds.

Best Strategy: The flop is four of diamonds, eight of spades, jack of diamonds. If you were the bettor in the left foreground, you would need a very strong hand to call the raise. As an example, you might need two eights (giving you three eights) to consider calling. That's because the best hand you could beat would be two fours (giving your opponent three fours). And two fours might be the minimum raising hand of some conservative opponents. You must ask yourself whether this opponent would have risked moving all-in with a jack and an eight (making two big pair) or a jack and a four. Liberal players might even raise all-in with a pair of aces or an ace of diamonds with an eight of diamonds. But, in that case, it's unlikely they'd perform the long *act* of deciding. If a raise truly is marginal, players are generally hesitant to let you know it. Here's an opportunity to earn a profit by throwing away some pretty good hands. Remember, what you save by not calling this raise is real money and it can buy real things.

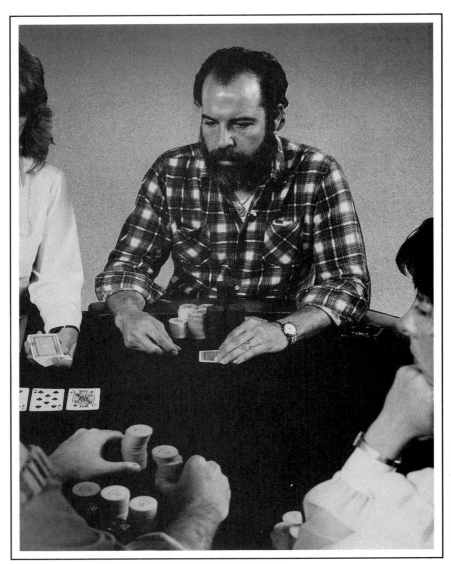

Photo 62: It's no-limit hold 'em and the man in the foreground is betting.

Photo by Lee McDonald

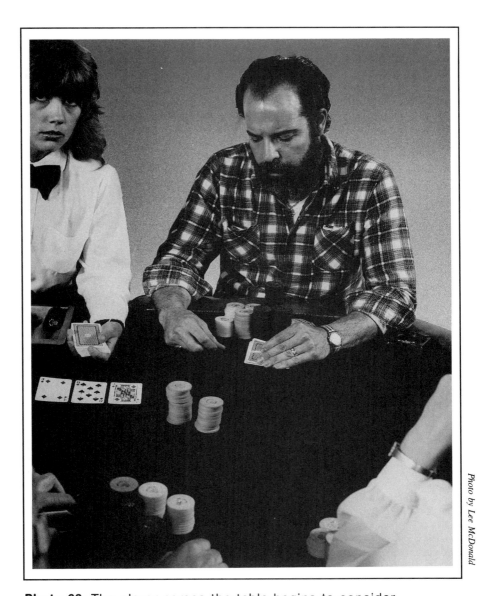

Photo by Lee McDonald

Photo 63: The player across the table begins to consider.

Continued

111

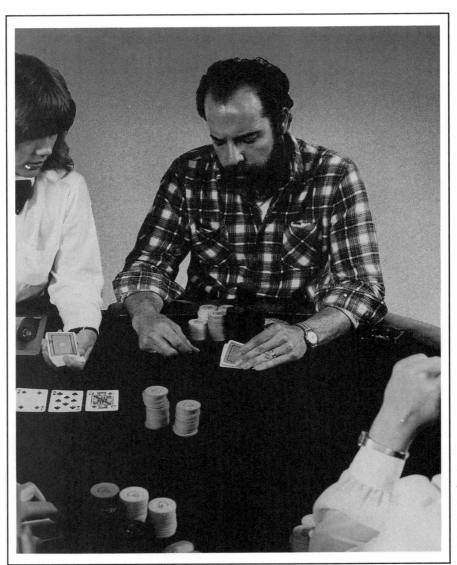

Photo by Lee McDonald

Photo 64: Ten seconds pass and he's still considering.

Photo by Lee McDonald

Photo 65: Now he puts a finger to his head to help his concentration.

Continued

113

Photo by Lee McDonald

Photo 66: Decision finally made, he gestures, "I've got it!"

Photo 67: He reaches for his stacks...

Continued

Photo 68: . . . and bets everything!

Chapter 13

Strong Means Weak

I often teach my students to concentrate on this aspect of tells first. In a poker game, the urge to act strong when weak can be overpowering for most players. Its reverse—weak when strong, which we've just studied—is also widespread.

You've seen, in terms of dollars, how much you can earn every hour by catching strong players in their tireless act of pretending to be weak.

But catching players who are pretending to be strong is even more valuable. The reason is simple. If you use the science of tells to determine that a player is strong, you'll often end up passing when you otherwise might have called. In a typical limit game, a pot may be $100 large and it would cost you $20 to call. If you discover that your opponent has a strong hand, you'll be able to fold with confidence. The most you will earn on a single tell is probably $20, the size of the saved bet. Of course, you can occasionally save two or more bets by folding even earlier in the hand. But, in an example where you're focusing on one late bet and deciding whether or not to call, $20 is usually the most you can save by correctly throwing your hand away.

It turns out that your *actual* savings is *less* than $20. That's because you might have decided to pass without even observing the tell. Also, the tell is not apt to be 100% accurate, so it might sometimes cause you to throw away a *winning* hand when you might otherwise have called. All in all, the information you gain by observing tells is healthy for your bankroll, but you must be aware that the theoretical value of each tell-related decision is apt to be only a percentage of what you think it is.

When you determine that a player is acting weak when strong, you'll often save a call, but the value is usually only a theoretical portion of the bet. It's a different story if you catch a player acting strong when weak. You will often use that information to make a courageous call you would not otherwise have considered. In such a case, you will frequently win an *entire pot* you would have lost!

Before going on, it's a good time to remind you that the dollar values given for each tell should be carefully interpreted. First, remember that the value is only an approximation and may vary from game to game. Second, it represents the *maximum* you could earn on that specific tell if you spotted it every time it occurred. In practice, nobody can be aware of everything that goes on at a poker table. Third, in some respects the dollar value is *greater* than you'd think, because the value provided applies to the specific tell under scrutiny and does not include related tells suggested by the same mannerism.

Now let's discover a vastly important category of tells. Never forget that players will not waste energy making you think they're strong when they really are. Why should they?

Caro's Law of Tells #12

*Disappoint any player who, by acting strong,
is hoping you'll pass.*

─────────── **Photos 69 & 70** ───────────

Title: If these cards change, I'll be a witness.

Category: Strong Means Weak.

Description: The player's eyes fix on the flop in Photo 69. That doesn't tell us much, because almost all hold 'em players watch the flop. But in Photo 70, the player's eyes remain on the flop, and that fact could be important.

Motivation: He's trying to appear dangerous by showing interest in the flop.

Reliability:		
	Weak players =	72%
	Average players =	65%
	Strong players =	55%

Value Per Hour:		
	$1 limit =	$1.40
	$10 limit =	$2.90
	$100 limit =	$14.00

Discussion: Players have a habit of continuing to stare at a flop they don't like. In their mind, by pretending to be interested, they're discouraging opponents from betting. It may even work—except against you. Being educated in the science of tells, you realize that players who like flops are likely to look away. If you notice that sometimes a player turns his head quickly away from the flop and sometimes he doesn't, you can figure he's weak whenever he continues to stare.

Best Strategy: Here's a good bluffing opportunity for you. Also, if this guy bets, you should call more liberally than usual, because there's a large chance that he's weak or bluffing.

Photo by Frank Mirani

Photo 69: The hold 'em player at left watches as the flop is spread.

Photo by Frank Mirani

Photo 70: His eyes remain on the flop.

--- **Photo 71**---

Title: Watch me make a fist.

Category: Strong Means Weak.

Description: Many novice players, and some intermediate players, try to fool the opposition by gesturing to rap pat before it's their turn. You can see the player second from right performing this act. There is no penalty for changing his mind, because general poker rules dictate that "acting out of turn is not binding."

Motivation: He hopes the opener will be mislead.

Reliability: Weak players = 88%
                      Average players = 68%
                      Strong players = 56%

Value Per Hour: $1 limit = $0.18
                         $10 limit = $1.10
                         $100 limit = $9.50

Discussion: Even if you can interpret this tell correctly, it seldom does you much good in high-hand-wins draw poker. True, the opponent is trying to mislead you by pretending to rap pat, but his motive is fairly hazy. He wants to fool you, but in his heart he doesn't quite know why. You can be fairly certain that he'll draw cards, but what can you do about it? In lowball, the tell is more beneficial (see *Best Strategy* which follows).

Best Strategy: If an opponent is pretending to rap pat behind you and your jacks-or-better-to-open hand is. . .

. . .you should definitely draw three to the aces and not be tricked into splitting openers and trying for the flush. If the game is lowball, there's a much greater chance that you can earn a profit here. If you have a hand such as 9-7-6-4-2 and were tempted to draw one, you should now rap pat, knowing that your lowball opponent will be drawing cards.

Photo 71: It's draw poker. The opener (second from left) is drawing a card while an opponent seems to be rapping pat.

——————————— **Photo 72** ———————————

Title: I'm watching, so you better know what you're doing.

Category: Strong Means Weak.

Description: Keep in mind that players looking *at* the bettor are typically less of a threat than players looking *away.* Here, the player at center is watching the bet.

Motivation: By appearing interested, he's trying to tell his opponent that a bet is not safe.

Reliability: Weak players = 70%
                Average players = 65%
                Strong players = 58%

Value Per Hour: $1 limit = $1.30
                $10 limit = $9.85
                $100 limit = $58.50

Discussion: While this is a fairly powerful tell, it has its problems. It's clear that players who stare at you are generally weaker than those who stare away. But it so happens that, especially in limit games, there's a secondary reason why opponents watch your bet: They want to make sure you wager the right amount, so they won't get short-changed. You can sometimes be fooled into thinking an opponent is trying to act strong when, in fact, he's only monitoring the size of your bet. This tell poses that dilemma. If the player (center) was looking directly at the bettor's face, we'd have no problem. In such a case, it would be fairly clear that the bet was unwelcome. Even in this photo, however, you can assume that the opponent watching the bet is not *usually* strong. Just for contrast, look at Photo 51 in Chapter 12, *Weak Means Strong.*

Best Strategy: You can bet medium-strength hands into the player at center with the hope of getting a call from a weaker hand. Also, if you hold a hopeless hand, you might try bluffing.

Caro's Law of Tells #13
*Players staring at you are usually less
of a threat than players staring away.*

Photo 72: Watch the man at center as his opponent (second from left) wagers.

─────────────── **Photos 73, 74 & 75** ───────────────

Title: I'll just keep staring until they get better.

Category: Strong Means Weak.

Description: If you've been in draw poker games against weak players, you've probably observed this. The player would normally guard his hand if he liked its looks. Now, however, he just stares at the cards as they arrive and, finally, in Photo 75 he reaches for his chips as if to bet.

Motivation: He's hoping players with medium hands will decide not to open. (If no one opens in jacks-or-better draw, there's traditionally a second ante and all players get a new chance at the pot.)

Reliability:
Weak players = 88%
Average players = 73%
Strong players = 62%

Value Per Hour:
$1 limit = $2.74
$10 limit = $18.50
$100 limit = $128.00

Discussion: In jacks-or-better-to-open draw poker, each player gets a chance to open the pot. If nobody opens, the antes remain in the pot and new antes are usually added. Then there's a brand new deal and everyone gets a second opportunity to win. If you held a garbage hand, obviously it would be to your advantage if no one opened. And that's exactly how the guy (right foreground) has it figured. By reaching for his chips out of turn and staring at his cards, he's hoping to convince his opponents that he's a threat. Maybe that will prevent them from opening with marginal hands. This seldom works, but players try anyway. The information you gain by observing their futile attempts can be very valuable. For comparison, see Photos 52, 53 and 54 in Chapter 12, *Weak Means Strong.*

Best Strategy: Not only should you go right ahead and open with any hand that seems marginal, you should open with some hands you might otherwise not have considered. The reason is that, in all forms of poker, the more players remaining to act behind you, the more jeopardy you're in. The fewer players remaining, the more liberally you can open. When you see a player behind you stare at his cards and reach for his chips, you should act as if he isn't there! You have fewer players to contend with and you can profit with hands you would not have played.

Caro's Law of Tells #14

Players staring at their cards are usually weak.

Caro's Law of Tells #15

*Players reaching for their
chips out of turn are usually weak.*

Photo by Raiko Hartman

Photo 73: It's draw poker high-hand-wins and the player at right foreground picks up three awful-looking cards.

Photo 74: Continuing to gaze at the first three cards held in his left hand, he picks up two more terrible cards.

Photo 75: He now stares at all five cards and reaches for his chips.

—————————————————— **Photo 76** ——————————————————

Title: I thought you already passed.

Category: Strong Means Weak.

Description: Here the bettor is reaching for the chips before her opponent has surrendered.

Motivation: She wants to show strength by indicating that the outcome is a sure thing.

Reliability: Weak players   = 85%
                  Average players = 81%
                  Strong players = 54%

Value Per Hour: $1 limit   = $0.90
                   $10 limit = $8.10
                   $100 limit = $7.50

Discussion: Strong players sometimes reach for the pot prematurely as a ploy to induce a call. (That's why this tell has a small proportional value in big-limit games.) Often, this is done ostentatiously while an opponent is just beginning to consider. However, when a player reaches for the pot while the opponent is *in the act of passing,* the interpretation is different. Usually, the bettor wants to ensure that the pot is won by driving the last tiny doubts from the mind of an already-passing opponent. While this may be difficult to conceptualize at first, consider that any player who truly holds a winning hand would give you every opportunity to call. If this woman wanted a call, she wouldn't reach for the pot until there was no chance whatsoever that you might change your mind.

Best Strategy: If you were about to throw your hand away, consider calling—even with a fairly weak hand. And if you have a hand so horrible that you can't beat anything, try raising as a bluff. Here's a chance to snare a whole pot that would have got away.

Caro's Law of Tells #16
*A weak player who gathers a pot prematurely
is usually bluffing.*

Photo by Raiko Hartman

Photo 76: The woman has bet and now, while the opponent at right is still in the act of passing, she begins to gather the pot.

———————————— **Photos 77, 78 & 79** ————————————

Title: Are you sure you want to call these?

Category: Strong Means Weak.

Description: Here we see a bet made in Photo 77. In Photo 78, the bettor stares at his cards. When his opponent begins to call, in Photo 79, the bettor quickly acts as if to spread a winning hand.

Motivation: He's desperately hoping to prevent the call.

Reliability:
          Weak players = 99%
          Average players = 89%
          Strong players = 78%

Value Per Hour:
          $1 limit = $1.32
          $10 limit = $9.04
          $100 limit = $52.00

Discussion: As a last futile, desperate effort to prevent a call, many players will start to spread a bluff (or a weak hand) on the table. You can actually elicit this tell by reaching for your chips and then gauging the reaction of a player who has bet into you. If he starts to spread his hand prematurely, you can be pretty certain that you can profitably make the call. I like to apply this tactic when I'm leaning toward passing. If I reach for my chips and the bettor starts to spread his hand, I'll just continue to make the call smoothly. Otherwise, I'll pass. Often you can salvage an entire pot because a player will apply this fairly common mannerism in an attempt to prevent you from betting.

Best Strategy: Call. And if you can't win calling, raise.

Caro's Law of Tells #17

When a player acts to spread his hand prematurely, it's usually because he's bluffing.

Photo by Raiko Hartman

Photo 77: The player in the hat wagers while his opponent (left) waits.

Photo by Raiko Hartman

Photo 78: The bettor now stares at his hand.

Continued

Photo by Raiko Hartman

Photo 79: As the opponent begins to call, the bettor starts to spread his hand face up on the table.

---------------------------- **Photos 80, 81 & 82** ----------------------------

Title: I was drawing for a straight! How can *you* bet?

Category: Strong Means Weak.

Description: I'll bet you've seen this before. The seven-stud player in the foreground tries for a straight in Photo 80, misses in Photo 81 and reaches for his chips while staring at his hole cards in Photo 82.

Motivation: He's hoping to prevent the bet in progress.

Reliability: Weak players = 93%
                       Average players = 84%
                        Strong players = 72%

Value Per Hour: $1 limit = $1.55
                          $10 limit = $9.00
                         $100 limit = $96.00

Discussion: Staring at seven-stud hole cards is somewhat rare in public casinos, but it happens a lot in home games. The more important thing to focus on is that the player in the foreground is reaching for his chips. You should already understand that the gesture is purely an effort to prevent a bet. There are all sorts of applications of the tell pictured, depending on whether you're the bettor or the man to the dealer's right. But wait! There's another terrific tell that you might have missed. The player to the dealer's right is looking back at his cards while the bet is in progress. This almost always means weakness! Players with strong hands may occasionally double-check, but only briefly. If a player who was *not already* staring at his cards begins to do so in the middle of an opponent's bet, he's doing it because he wants to be seen. Specifically, he's hoping to appear threatening. We can carry this concept further. If someone has bet and then looks back at his cards as you reach toward your chips to call, there's an overwhelming chance that he's bluffing.

Best Strategy: If you're the bettor, continue with the wager. You might get called by the player in the foreground who missed the straight (he also has a pair of nines). Alternately, you might choose to check if you think that the chances of gaining a call are slim but that one of your opponents might try to bluff. You could then call and win an extra bet.

Caro's Law of Tells #18

If a player bets and then looks back at his hand as you reach for your chips, he's probably bluffing.

Photo by Lee McDonald

Photo 80: The seven-stud player in the foreground requires a ten or a five to complete a straight.

Photo by Lee McDonald

Photo 81: No help.

Photo by Lee McDonald

Photo 82: As an opponent bets, the player stares at his hole cards and reaches for his chips.

Chapter 14

Exposing Cards

Careless players sometimes expose cards by accident. This usually happens when they aren't interested in the pot. A player who's involved in a betting war or is otherwise competing for a pot will usually guard a hand carefully. When you see a player expose one or more strong cards, beware! Also, though this is rare, a player may expose a weak card when he holds a powerful hand. In either case, the exposure is seldom accidental.

You can correctly suppose that a player who deliberately exposes a strong card or several strong cards is actually weak. Let's take a look...

───────────────────── **Photo 83** ─────────────────────

Title: Try figuring out what three cards I'm keeping.

Category: Exposing Cards.

Description: This is draw poker with a pair of jacks minimum required to open. The player in the center is the opener. His opponent, who first passed and later called the opening bet, is at left. When this photo was taken, the caller had already drawn three cards, probably to a pair smaller than jacks. The opener is now drawing two cards while "accidentally" exposing a ten.

Motivation: He wants to make his opponent think he has three tens.

Reliability:	Weak players	=	92%
	Average players	=	83%
	Strong players	=	71%

Value Per Hour:	$1 limit	=	$0.30
	$10 limit	=	$1.50
	$100 limit	=	$4.80

Discussion: The opener is hoping that the caller will use some simple logic. Since at least a pair of jacks is required to open, it seems more likely that the exposed ten indicates three tens than a higher pair with a ten kicker. But if this guy really had three tens, he wouldn't want to let anyone know—especially his opponent. Rather, he'd hope the opponent would help his small pair (making three eights, for instance) and then call. It's important to understand what the opener seeks to accomplish. He probably holds a pair of jacks, queens or kings and doesn't want the opponent to bet two pair or even three of a kind. If the opponent improves and doesn't bet, the opener may still lose the pot, but it won't cost him any more money. This whole act of exposing a ten is designed to stop the opponent from betting. Therefore, the exposed ten is intended as a *strong* card, which you know means the opposite.

Under other circumstances, if the opponent hadn't first passed and then "backed in" to call, the opener might suspect the caller has a better hand than his weak openers. In such a case, he might expose the ten and then *bet*, hoping the opponent would throw away the better hand. In this photo, he will no doubt check unless he improves. Remember, the opener figures to have the best hand so far, but it's a vulnerable hand and he doesn't want to have to consider calling a bet.

Best Strategy: What can I tell you? If you're the player at left and called with a pair of eights, you probably made a mistake! Calling with a small pair is simply not profitable in most situations. Still, here you are contending for the pot, so what can you do now? Well, if the opener checks and you make *any* two pair, you should bet. A bet is what the opener is trying to prevent, so why make him happy? Also, this is a very good bluffing opportunity if you *don't* help your hand.

Photo by Raiko Hartman

Photo 83: The player at center is asking for two cards and exposing a ten among the three cards he's keeping.

139

——————————— **Photo 84** ———————————

Title: It's too much trouble betting with my left hand.

Category: Exposing Cards.

Description: The player in the foreground is holding his cards in the same hand he's using to make his bet. This causes the "accidental" exposure of the joker.

Motivation: He wants to convey strength.

Reliability:	Weak players	= 84%
	Average players	= 75%
	Strong players	= 61%

Value Per Hour:	$1 limit	= $0.90
	$10 limit	= $3.00
	$100 limit	= $14.00

Discussion: The inclusion of the joker, making the deck 53 cards deep, is common in draw poker. Sometimes the joker is considered a wild card which can represent anything the holder desires; sometimes (as with legal games in California) it's limited to use as an ace or to complete a straight or a flush. In any case, it's a powerful card. Ask yourself why an opponent would want to expose a joker while betting. There's something wrong, isn't there? He must be attempting to trick you into thinking he's strong when he's weak. This is probably a bluff.

Best Strategy: Call.

Chapter 15

Opening Tells

Determining who's going to open a pot and who isn't is one of the most profitable applications of tells. In games where you can check and later call or raise, there's seldom a reason for you to make the first bet if someone else will do it for you.

The advantages in knowing whether someone intends to open are many. If you were considering playing a weak hand, you can bow out gracefully by simply checking and later passing. If you have a strong hand, it's usually better to check, let the opponent open and see how many callers there are by the time the action returns to your position. At that point you can either call or raise. In fact, there may be several raises by the time the action returns, and this may indicate your hand is not worth playing. In such a case, you can pass without losing even an opening bet.

Opening tells are extremely powerful in many forms of poker. They are most common in draw poker games. That's because in high-hand-wins draw poker, there's an incentive for players to disguise their hands even if they have no chance of winning. If nobody opens, the original ante is not lost—there is a double ante and a new deal. That's motive enough for players who are holding weak hands to pretend to be strong, thereby keeping you from opening.

Here are seven players. . .

———————————— **Photo 85** ————————————

Title: To open or not to open...

Category: Opening Tells.

Description: It's draw poker, jacks-or-better to open. The player in the foreground (left) holds three aces, but he'd just as soon let someone else open. Someone will. Which player is it?

Motivation: The player who will open is trying to appear as if he isn't a threat.

Reliability:	Weak players	=	98%
	Average players	=	91%
	Strong players	=	80%

Value Per Hour:	$1 limit	=	$2.18
	$10 limit	=	$11.20
	$100 limit	=	$85.00

Discussion: It's up to the player holding three aces to either check or open. He wants to know if anyone else will bet for him, so let's go clockwise around the table and find out. First, there's a man who's reaching for his chips out of turn. He's trying to suggest he has a hand strong enough to open; therefore he probably doesn't. Then there's a woman staring at her cards, trying to make us think they're powerful. Since strong means weak, she must have less than the minimum pair of jacks required to open. Next, a man is gazing away from the action and even pretending to throw his hand away. There's an overwhelming chance that he'll open. Weak means strong, remember. If you hold the three aces, you'd know not to open because this man will do it for you. The last three players are all staring at their cards and probably have weak hands.

Best Strategy: If you have the three aces in the foreground, check and let the man in the leather jacket open. By the way, his mannerisms suggest that he has a pretty powerful hand, so deciding whether you should raise or just call will be difficult.

Photo 85: The cards have just been dealt and these seven players are competing for the jacks-or-better pot.

Chapter 16

Encouraging Your Bet

When players encourage your bet, it's because they think they have a winning hand. Some of the usual ways of luring bets are not visual, but audible. They're related to the act of conveying weakness through tone of voice, sighs and other sounds. We'll deal with that in *Part Four— The Sounds of Tells*.

The most common visual methods opponents use to make your bet appear safe are: (1) Looking away as if uninterested; (2) Pretending to pass; and (3) Keeping their hands off their chips.

——————————————— **Photo 86** ———————————————

Title: I wonder if it's raining in Cincinnati.

Category: Encouraging Your Bet.

Description: At left, a man is considering his bet. At center, an opponent studies seriously. Focus on the man at right. He's acting as if he isn't even involved. Maybe you don't consider him a threat, but you should.

Motivation: The man at right wants to do nothing to interfere with a possible bet.

Reliability: Weak players = 96%
                     Average players = 91%
                     Strong players = 69%

Value Per Hour: $1 limit = $2.04
                          $10 limit = $14.60
                         $100 limit = $95.00

Discussion: Since the man at center looks so studious, you should figure that he doesn't have a powerhouse. If he did, he'd be apt to encourage your bet by appearing uninterested. Here he either has a genuine tough decision or he's trying to intimidate his opponent into passing. Yes, close scrutiny can be intimidating. The man at right is strong. Whenever you see an active player looking as if the pot is far from his mind. . .well, that's a dangerous opponent. In all probability, he's hoping for a bet and, in response, he'll raise.

Best Strategy: Pass, unless you have a powerful hand. Even then, you should probably check and let him do the betting. Don't bluff.

Photo by Cliff Stanley

Photo 86: The player at left is considering a bet while one man studies and another looks bored.

——————————— **Photo 87** ———————————

Title: Can't you see I'm going to pass?

Category: Encouraging Your Bet.

Description: In the previous tell, you saw a man looking away. This man is also looking away, but, additionally, he's getting ready to throw his cards away. Or so you're supposed to presume.

Motivation: He's hungry for your bet.

Reliability:
    Weak players = 100%
    Average players = 94%
    Strong players = 90%

Value Per Hour:
    $1 limit = $3.50
    $10 limit = $20.40
    $100 limit = $185.00

Discussion: There's not much to say here. Study that man across the table. He's looking away *and* beginning to pass out of turn. This is an outstanding example of what real-life players do to encourage your bet. Whenever you see this, you're in a lot more trouble than you can itemize.

Best Strategy: Don't bet. When he bets, pass. Don't bluff. Don't expect to catch him bluffing. One note about finesse: Since this tell is so valuable, you should not pass instantly. Your decision is obvious, but don't make it *seem* obvious to your opponent. If you do, he might change his behavior and provide fewer tells in the future. If you hesitate before making your decision, he'll figure that his act almost worked—and he may even exaggerate it the next time.

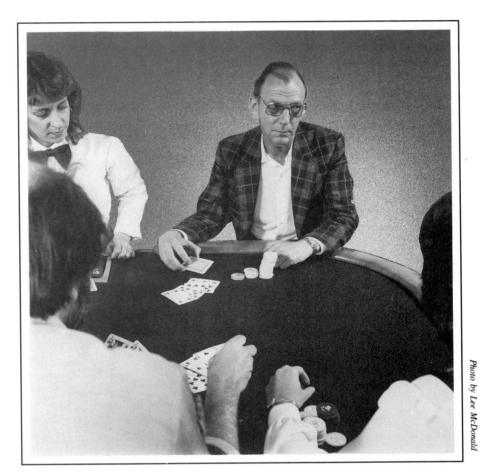

Photo by Lee McDonald

Photo 87: The player in the right foreground is betting. Is the bet safe?

---------------------------------- **Photo 88** ----------------------------------

Title: Never worry about a girl like me.

Category: Encouraging Your Bet.

Description: While the man bets, the woman in the black sweater very subtly stares at the table, unwilling to move. Her left hand provides a slight hint that she might be passing.

Motivation: She doesn't want to discourage the bet.

Reliability: Weak players = 88%
                Average players = 80%
                Strong players = 72%

Value Per Hour: $1 limit = $2.08
                $10 limit = $11.00
                $100 limit = $50.00

Discussion: It would be nice if all tells were as blatant as those shown in the two previous photos. Many are, but some are much more subtle. Take Photo 88, for instance. This is composed of the same elements that made up the previous tell. But here it's harder to spot. The woman *is* looking away, but she isn't gazing off the table or into space. She's simply looking down. Don't be fooled into thinking she's staring at her chips. Instinctive glances at chips, which we've already studied, are extremely brief, and they occur when your opponent is not aware that you're looking. In any case, they lead you to the same conclusion—the woman holds a strong hand.

A long, unmoving stare coupled with no threatened call means the woman is simply focusing away from the action in an effort to make the bet seem safe. If you study closely, you'll also see that this player is holding her cards in a gesture slightly indicative of a pass. You must not be mislead by the subtleness of this tell. She is trying to encourage a bet. And the most likely reason a player would want to encourage a bet is because he or she is about to raise.

Best Strategy: Don't bet into this player. Don't call without a very strong hand.

Photo by Raiko Hartman

Photo 88: The bet is coming from the man in the checked shirt. His opponent is the woman at right.

Chapter 17

Discouraging Your Bet

The advantage in knowing when an opponent is trying to *encourage* your bet is this: You can save the money or chips you would have otherwise wagered. That's because most times you won't have a hand big enough to either bet or call against an apparently strong hand. Even if you do have a fairly big hand, you can simply check now and call later. That way, you won't wager first and then be faced with calling a surprise raise.

The advantage in knowing when an opponent is trying to *discourage* your bet is different: You can earn extra money or chips by betting marginal hands in the hope of getting called by hands that are even weaker. There is another great advantage: You can sometimes bluff into the player with a reasonable chance of success. Keep in mind that players holding weaker-than-average hands are less likely to call than players holding hands of unknown strength. Players who are trying to discourage your bet usually have weaker-than-average hands.

One more thing. Just as with the tells relating to players who are trying to encourage your bet, you'll seldom see a tell as blatant as the one in the next photograph. Though the signs may be more subtle, search and you'll find them. But even the *exact* tell photographed will be seen occasionally.

———————————— **Photo 89** ————————————

Title: How much do you want to bet, sucker?

Category: Discouraging Your Bet.

Description: It's seven stud. The woman is looking at the bettor and grabbing for her stack of chips. Both of these mannerisms are important.

Motivation: She is trying to make her opponent change his mind about betting.

Reliability:		
	Weak players	= 97%
	Average players	= 91%
	Strong players	= 73%

Value Per Hour:		
	$1 limit	= $1.02
	$10 limit	= $7.30
	$100 limit	= $51.00

Discussion: Study the woman across the table. Among beginning and intermediate players, this is a common method of trying to prevent a bet. The reason players want to stop you from betting is because they hold weak hands with some possibility of winning. In other words, they'd like to see both hands shown down on the table. Then maybe they can salvage the pot. Reaching for chips is intended to show strength and appear threatening. As you now know, players staring at you are less of a threat than those staring away. So here we have a classic example of a woman combining two tells that point in the same direction (looking at the bettor and reaching for her chips). She is probably holding a marginally weak hand.

This gives you opportunities to bet hands you would have otherwise checked. The seven stud hand in the foreground is an ideal example of a hand you should bet. It's two pair, jacks over sevens. The opponent has a pair of tens on the board and three small hearts. You should know better than to worry about the flush, because if she had it, she would *not* try to discourage your bet. There is some opportunity to bluff here, but be advised that there's a sexist consideration. You may not like to make generalizations, but within the science of tells generalizations spell profit. Take this one: In general, women who threaten to call are more likely to follow through and *actually* call than men. Men are more apt to remove fingers from their chips and simply throw their cards away. Therefore, when you see the mannerism pictured, you'll have better success bluffing into a man than into a woman.

Best Strategy: Bet marginal hands for value. Consider bluffing, but with caution.

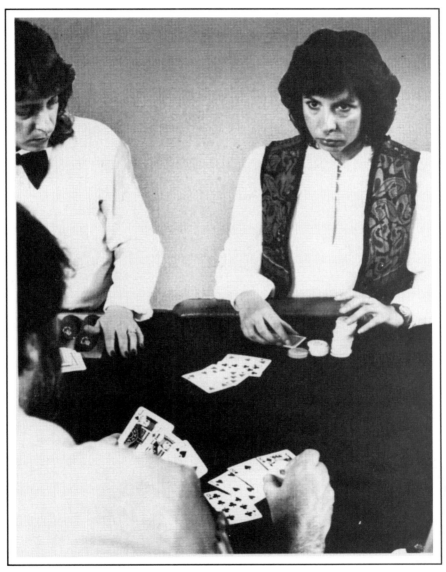

Photo by Lee McDonald

Photo 89: While the player in the foreground begins to bet, the woman across the table stares at him and reaches for her chips.

157

Chapter 18

Betting Moves

You can often determine the strength of a player's cards just by watching the way he bets. If a player wants a call, he'll be very careful not to frighten you. In his mind, overly forceful or exaggerated betting moves will make his hand appear strong. Bland, timid motions convey weakness, he thinks.

The key to interpreting your opponent's hand by the manner he bets is not very difficult. If the move is too dynamic or exaggerated, you should suspect weakness. If it's quiet and smooth, suspect strength.

When a player couples his wager with the words, "I bet," or something similar in an optimistic or authoritative tone, there's a good chance he's weak or bluffing. If he says nothing or announces his bet in a negative tone, figure him for a strong hand.

In a sense, the whole science of interpreting betting moves runs contrary to what you might at first expect. You've already learned that players who are bluffing or weak often try to blend in with the tablecloth after betting (see *Part One—Tells From Those Who Are Unaware,* Chapter 4, titled *Nervousness).* Then, shouldn't you expect a player who's bluffing to bet in a very sedate manner so as not to call attention to himself?

No. The reason is that bluffers try to disappear only after their bet. At that time they're not required to do anything but sit and await their fate. While waiting, they try to do nothing that might trigger your call. But while betting, they don't have the luxury of doing nothing. No matter what they might desire, they know they're sure to call attention to themselves while placing the bet. That's why they revert to trying to disguise their hands the only way they know how. They act weak when strong and strong when weak.

Betting with extra emphasis is an attempt to appear strong. It means weak. Betting casually is an attempt to appear weak. It means strong. A casual bet is frequently accompanied by other overt signs of pretended weakness: shrugging, sighing and negative tones of voice.

Sometimes you must be cautious. While a dynamic bet usually means weakness, a few players—particularly sophisticated opponents—will bet with a great deal of force in an attempt to intimidate you into calling. This is how you can tell the difference: A bluff is usually bet with *slightly* or *moderately* too much force and is generally directed at nobody in particular (or at a player who poses little threat); a strong hand might occasionally be bet with overwhelming force, but that bet will be aimed *specifically* at an opponent who seems to hold a strong hand, and the demeanor of the bettor may well be defiant.

This section is intended as a guide for deciphering the hands of players who *vary* their betting moves. The forthcoming photos will be of little use if you play only against players who use the same betting move all the time.

Caro's Law of Tells #19

A forceful or exaggerated bet usually means weakness.

Caro's Law of Tells #20

A gentle bet usually means strength.

—————————— Photos 90, 91 & 92 ——————————

Title: Don't let this bet scare you.

Category: Betting Moves.

Description: The player gently slides his bet into the pot.

Motivation: He's hoping for a call and doesn't want to intimidate his opponent.

Reliability:		
	Weak players	= 79%
	Average players	= 71%
	Strong players	= 63%

Value Per Hour:		
	$1 limit	= $0.90
	$10 limit	= $6.05
	$100 limit	= $14.00

Discussion: Sliding chips is an ideal example of a betting motion chosen by players who hold strong hands and are hoping for calls. Players with weak hands typically feel the need to add extra flair to bolster their bets. This pattern isn't perfect. Occasionally a player may decide to make a timid bluff, but that's rare. If you find such a player, remember his or her move so you can capitalize next time it occurs. Mostly, players who bet softly have the goods. One big word of caution here. Some players always use the same betting move no matter what. If they always slide their chips in the same way, bluffing or not, then you shouldn't apply this tell.

Best Strategy: Don't call without a powerful hand.

Photo by Lee McDonald

Photo 90: The player (center) begins to bet with his right hand.

Photo by Lee McDonald

Photo 91: He continues to push the chips forward toward the pot.

Photo 92: He completes the bet and casually withdraws his fingers.

—————————— **Photo 93** ——————————

Title: If you call this, you're crazy!

Category: Betting Moves.

Description: The bettor dances these chips into the pot. Notice his arm reaching far forward. One finger is stiff, indicating that he's attaching a little extra force to the departing chips.

Motivation: He's weak and hopes his bet will be too intimidating to call.

Reliability:
Weak players = 98%
Average players = 94%
Strong players = 80%

Value Per Hour:
$1 limit = $2.81
$10 limit = $22.65
$100 limit = $183.00

Discussion: Always look for an extended forearm. When you can see almost no bend at the elbow, there's a good chance of a bluff. That happens only rarely, but the action of flinging chips in with a somewhat exaggerated fingertip motion is typical of a bluffer. There's another tell here. The player at right is leaning back and looking at his cards for the first time as the bet is made. If he were leaning forward or paying attention to the bettor, we'd suspect he was acting to prevent a bet by giving the impression he held something powerful. This posture is somewhat different, though, and it makes for a difficult tell. A good theory is that this is genuine indecision. He's probably drawn one card, perhaps to a flush. Now he's squeezing out his hand to see if he made it.

Best Strategy: Call this bettor. If you can't win in a showdown, raise.

Photo 93: Study the bettor (left).

—————————————— **Photo 94** ——————————————

Title: You've got nothing to worry about, fella.

Category: Betting Moves.

Description: Compare this photo to Photo 93 of the previous tell. The difference is this: The bettor isn't extending his forearm nearly as far; he's not using his fingertips to emphasize his bet; and he's about to put his chips in gently rather than flinging them.

Motivation: He doesn't want to frighten away the potential caller.

Reliability: Weak players = 91%
                      Average players = 84%
                       Strong players = 70%

Value Per Hour: $1 limit = $1.50
                            $10 limit = $8.14
                           $100 limit = $22.00

Discussion: Players who bet gently are likely to hold big hands. In truth, there are occasionally *very* gentle bets that turn out to be bluffs. In such cases, players are afraid that extra emphasis will lure a call. However, that's rare. By and large, players who bet gently are strong, and you'll make a lot of money if you consider that the case until they demonstrate otherwise. Also, there's a secondary tell at work. The player at right is doing nothing to discourage this bet. You guessed it! He's ready to pounce, so expect a raise.

Best Strategy: Don't call this bet with anything but a respectable hand.

Photo by Allen Photographers

Photo 94: Here the bettor's forearm is not extended as much, and he appears to be placing the chips in more gently.

—————————————— **Photo 95** ——————————————

Title: Nobody ever called a bet like this and lived to tell about it!

Category: Betting Moves.

Description: The woman is flinging her bet into the pot.

Motivation: She's weak and wants to appear strong.

Reliability: Weak players = 87%
                   Average players = 71%
                    Strong players = 54%

Value Per Hour: $1 limit = $2.40
                      $10 limit = $11.00
                     $100 limit = $44.30

Discussion: Anytime you see a really exaggerated bet, such as the one this woman is making during a seven-stud hand, you should ask yourself this question: Is she betting at anyone in particular? If the answer is yes, there's some chance that she's using the maneuver as a challenge to lure a call. If the answer is no, as it is in this photo, then the betting move is an attempt to show strength and therefore you should suspect that the woman is weak or bluffing.

Best Strategy: Call this bet if you have any reasonable hand at all. If you don't, raise as fast as you can—she might pass before you get your chips in!

Photo 95: This woman is making an exaggerated bet.

Chapter 19

Tricks

Opponents are always trying to outsmart you. If you're confident that an opponent is acting, remember to ask yourself what he hopes to accomplish. Usually, the answer is astonishingly simple.

Here are two examples of players trying to fool their opponents...

——————————————— **Photo 96** ———————————————

Title: You better call quick before I take this pot.

Category: Tricks.

Description: The player at left has made a bet. While the opponent at center deliberates, the bettor makes a sweeping gesture to corral the pot. His arms will often remain outstretched until the opponent makes up his mind.

Motivation: He's trying to lure a call by using such strange behavior that his opponent will become suspicious.

Reliability:	Weak players	=	64%
	Average players	=	58%
	Strong players	=	52%

Value Per Hour:	$1 limit	=	$0.07
	$10 limit	=	$0.51
	$100 limit	=	$2.02

Discussion: While this may look similar to the tell discussed earlier in Chapter 13, *Strong Means Weak* in this, *Part Two—Tells From Actors* (Photo 76), it isn't. In that case the bettor grabbed for the chips while the opponent was passing, acting strong to keep him from reconsidering. Remember, players with winning hands will give an opponent every opportunity to call. What you see in Photo 96 is a ploy. The opponent hasn't even decided what to do yet. The bettor's hands remain outstretched while he awaits that decision. When you see a pot-snatching mannerism this blatant, you can be pretty sure the bettor wants his actions to appear bizarre. He figures that will earn him a call—and it usually does.

Best Strategy: Pass, unless you can beat a solid hand.

Photo 96: Here's a man reaching for a pot.

Photo by Raiko Hartman

———————— Photos 97, 98 & 99 ————————

Title: Look! I'm betting no matter what!

Category: Tricks.

Description: In this sequence, the player seems to look and bet at the same time.

Motivation: He wants his action to appear suspicious enough to lure a call.

Reliability:
Weak players = 60%
Average players = 66%
Strong players = 83%

Value Per Hour:
$1 limit = $0.13
$10 limit = $1.10
$100 limit = $12.50

Discussion: This is one of those rare tells that works better against strong players than against weak players. Sometimes, particularly in draw poker or seven stud (as shown), you'll meet an opponent who looks at the card or cards he's just caught (here, on seventh street) and prepares to bet at the same time. Many players find it suspicious when they encounter this movement. They feel bewildered and usually call the bet with weak hands. Wrong decision. When a player prepares to bet as he looks at his card, he's usually aware that his action will cause suspicion. In fact, he's using the tactic expressly to encourage a call. Because of that, he'll usually abandon his bet if he doesn't make a winning hand. Also, there's a good chance he *already* has the hand made and is looking and betting at the same time just to lure a call.

Best Strategy: Anytime you see a player seem to look at his card while beginning to bet, then complete his bet without hesitation, he's trying to fool you into thinking he would have bet no matter what. You need a very strong hand to call the bet pictured.

Photo by Lee McDonald

Photo 97: It's seven stud and this player is reaching for his chips as he begins to peek at his seventh and final card.

Continued

175

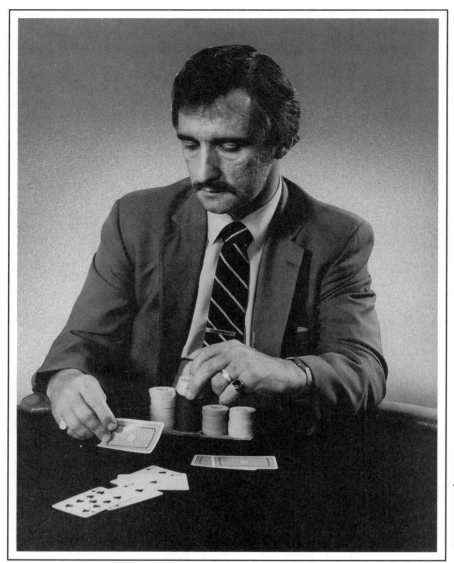

Photo 98: He continues the bet as he picks up the card.

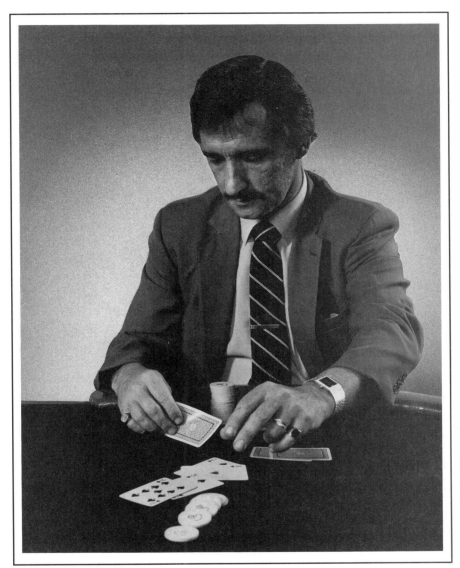

Photo 99: Smoothly he completes the bet.

Part Three

Some General Tells

Here is a collection of tells not specifically covered in the first two parts. You will discover many links between these and the mannerisms previously discussed. Still, each of the next four chapters deals with an important *new* aspect of tell science. For that reason, the concepts deserve to be studied separately.

Chapter 20

Choosing Your Seat

The seat you select in a poker game can do much to determine how much you'll earn. Many players choose their seats on the basis of hunches or superstition.

When there's a choice of chairs available, you can watch them stand near the table overwhelmed by the decision they must make. They wait, sometimes for ten seconds or more, until the inspiration strikes them. Then their spine tingles mysteriously, a mental arrow points the direction and they approach the lucky seat confidently.

Some people think superstition is silly and a seat's a seat. That's half right. Superstition is silly, but a seat is *not* a seat. Some are much better than others. Not only is seat selection important when you first enter a game, it's often profitable to *change* seats when a better one becomes available. Remember, poker action moves clockwise.

Some of the most valuable reasons for choosing a certain seat are not tell related. It's good to sit behind (to the left) of opponents who play too many pots but who are unaggressive. That way when you raise, these players will already have money invested. If you're on their right and raise, they probably won't play and you'll lose their action. Also, sit to the left of very aggressive, knowledgeable players. They can interfere with your strategy, so let them act first.

In games where there's a forced blind bet, there are two things to consider. First, it's good to be immediately to the right of a player who doesn't defend his blind by calling frequently enough. That way you can bet very weak hands when nobody else has entered the pot and you'll often win his blind and the antes without a fight. Second (and more important), sit to the left of players who are timid in attacking your blind. Since the nature of poker dictates that players in early positions must enter pots more selectively than those in late positions, the last players to act are often left with the opportunity of attacking your blind. If the players immediately to your right are timid, they'll often let you keep your blind and win the antes. That's a bonus for your bankroll.

All those considerations are hard to balance and often it's tough to determine the best seat on a purely strategic basis. Additionally, you may enter a game where you know little or nothing about the habits of the players.

In that case, there's an important tell you should know. . .

Caro's Law of Tells #21
When in doubt, sit behind the money.

––––––––––––––––––––––– **Photo 100** –––––––––––––––––––––––

Title: Where is the treasure buried?

Category: Choosing Your Seat.

Description: You have just approached this table. It's hold 'em and these opponents seem harmless enough. Should you take the chair in front of you or walk around the table to claim that vacant seat?

Motivation: You're trying to pick the most profitable seat.

Reliability:	Weak players	=	62%
	Average players	=	60%
	Strong players	=	58%

Value Per Hour:	$1 limit	=	$1.00
	$10 limit	=	$9.50
	$100 limit	=	$80.00

Discussion: If you take the seat in the foreground, you'll be better off. The key is the man at your right. He has a lot of chips and they're stacked haphazardly. This indicates he will probably be playing loose poker. Remember, you want to sit to the left of players who are loose, so, if you decide to raise, they'll already be in the pot. You certainly don't want to chase away their action by raising.

If the chips were stacked more neatly, your decision would be the same. You might then figure that this man is winning by skill and you'd just as soon see what he does before you act. In any case, you're about to sit in this game to earn a profit. Because of positional play in poker, you usually have more opportunities to win the money on your right than the money on your left or across the table. That's why, as a general rule, you should position as many chips on your right as possible.

Best Strategy: Take one step forward and sit right down.

Photo 100: There are two seats available. One's right in front of you and the other is at the far end of the table.

Chapter 21

Conflicting Tells

Oh, gee. Tells aren't always as clear as we'd like them to be. On rare occasions, you'll see two or more concurrent mannerisms that seem to suggest different things.

Relax. You can unscramble these mysteries fairly easily. In most cases, the opponent is aware of only *some* of his actions. He or she is acting, but it's not a whole-body act. Therefore, these dilemmas can be resolved simply by judging which mannerism is most likely to be an act.

If a man seems about to throw his cards away with one very visible gesture while his other hand is slyly creeping toward his chips, the puzzle is resolved. The hand doing the passing is the one he figures you're aware of. His *act* is that he's weak and about to surrender. The other hand is in the background and it's inching toward his chips. If that were an act, he'd make it more blatant—perhaps touching the top of his stacks in a claw-like manner.

There's really no reason to itemize the hundreds of common combinations of conflicting tells. Just be aware that when you see a conflict, it's probable one part of the player is acting and one part isn't. The act is whatever he thinks you're aware of. The rest is unconscious.

We could easily leave this section now, but there's one type of tell conflict that's extremely common and very profitable to observe. Wanna see it?

Caro's Law of Tells #22

When tells conflict, the player is acting. Determine what he's trying to make you do by his most blatant *mannerism. Then generally do the opposite.*

—————————————— **Photo 101** ——————————————

Title: I don't see you. Honest, I don't.

Category: Conflicting Tells.

Description: Here the man on the right does not want to discourage the bet. He won't look at the bettor directly, but his eyes tell a different story.

Motivation: He's hungry for this bet.

Reliability:
Weak players = 100%
Average players = 94%
Strong players = 85%

Value Per Hour:
$1 limit = $3.00
$10 limit = $18.00
$100 limit = $105.00

Discussion: Take a good look at the player in the dark shirt. This guy's going to raise. It's seven stud and his three exposed cards are six, nine, seven of mixed suits. In the hole he has an eight and a ten, providing him with a straight. Are you supposed to know that just by looking at the photo? Of course not! I peeked at his hand. What you *do* know is that this man has a very strong combination of cards and is seeking the bet. His head—that's the part he thinks his opponent may be conscious of—is locked straight ahead and he refuses to pose a threat by turning toward the bettor. But his eyes secretly monitor the action.

Best Strategy: Abandon this bet.

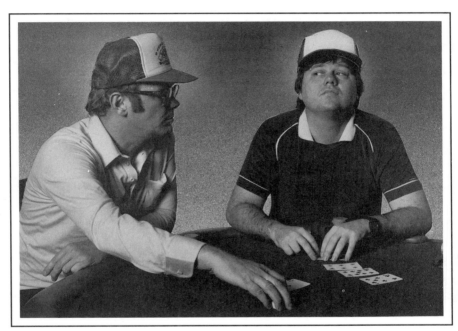

Photo by Frank Mitrani

Photo 101: The player at right is struggling to keep his face pointed away from the bet. But look at his eyes!

Photo 102

Title: I better not grab too soon.

Category: Conflicting Tells.

Description: In this case, the woman's eyes are watching the bet. However, that's not what she expects you to be aware of. Her head is turned away and she's practically passing with her left hand.

Motivation: She doesn't want to give the bettor anything to worry about.

Reliability:
    Weak players = 100%
    Average players = 96%
    Strong players = 90%

Value Per Hour:
    $1 limit = $3.05
    $10 limit = $24.50
    $100 limit = $190.00

Discussion: This common tell leaves no room for doubt. Her head *is* turned away—an act. She *is* acting as if to pass—an act. And her eyes *are* following the bet—*not* an act. Memorize this photo. You're looking at a woman who holds a very strong hand.

Best Strategy: Do not bet.

Photo by Cliff Stanley

Photo 102: Here's a more exaggerated variation of the previous tell.

Chapter 22

Gaining Information

Since tells are very valuable, it's beneficial to encourage them. If you can intimidate your opponents, they'll provide more and easier tells. This is a poker fact of life. Players who remain calm, rational and in control are better able to camouflage their hands.

If you play a powerful, aggressive, winning poker, your opponents will feel threatened. If you can convince them that you are master of your table, they will fight back with ill-conceived efforts designed to confuse you. These actions and reactions will be desperate and primitive: weak when strong, strong when weak. So, just by playing sensible, aggressive poker, you'll invite abundant tells.

Beyond that, there are specific things you can do in special situations to elicit tells. Here are some of them...

——————Photos 103, 104, 105 & 106 ——————

Title: A tale with two endings.

Category: Gaining Information.

Description: It's draw poker, jacks-or-better to open, and in Photo 103 the professional player at center takes three. In response, his opponent (the woman wearing the striped blouse) draws one card. At this point, the pro has made aces up. He would like to bet if the woman has two pair. But if, instead, she was drawing one to a straight or a flush, it would be senseless and dangerous to bet. So, in Photo 105 he pretends to bet and gets a threatening response. Photo 106 is a substitute ending for the same information-gathering maneuver. This time the woman's response is quite different.

Motivation: The professional is trying to gain information about the advisability of a bet.

Reliability: Weak players = 94%*
                   Average players = 83%*
                   Strong players = 64%*

*NOTE: These percentages of reliability apply to the response of the player at which the information-gaining ploy is aimed.

Value Per Hour: $1 limit = $1.69
                       $10 limit = $13.80
                       $100 limit = $84.00

Discussion: If the pro gets the response shown in Photo 105, he'll go right ahead and bet. The woman is threatening to call, so she's hoping he won't wager. Figure her for two small pair. In Photo 106, the woman looks away with that ubiquitous ready-to-pounce mannerism. She's made a straight, a flush or a full house—take my word for it. For that reason, the expert will check, allow the woman to bet, pretend to ponder, and then pass quietly without losing a single extra chip.

Best Strategy: If the rules of your game allow you to fake a bet without completing it, try this maneuver once in a while. Don't overdo it or your opponents will catch on.

Photo by Raiko Hartman

Photo 103: The professional at center draws three cards.

Photo by Raiko Hartman

Photo 104: His opponent in the striped blouse draws one.

Continued

Photo by Raiko Hartman

Photo 105: The professional reaches for his chips as if to bet and, in response, the woman grabs for her chips threateningly and fans her cards.

Photo by Raiko Hartman

Photo 106: But the professional might not have been answered with the response in Photo 105. He might have seen this instead.

——————— Photos 107, 108, 109 & 110 ———————

Title: Let me make sure.

Category: Gaining Information.

Description: When the player at left begins to bet, the professional decides to put him under a little pressure. He has no intention of calling so far, but if he gets the right tell. . .well, that's a different story. So, in the second photo (108), the pro reaches for his chips as if to call. This may look like the same bet-preventing move used by weak and average players, but it isn't. This is a professional ploy designed to yield valuable information. In this case (Photo 109), the pro causes the bettor to double-check his hand. Then (Photo 110), the bet is finally completed with greater-than-average force.

Motivation: The pro is planning to pass, but he's hoping to gain information that will save him the pot.

Reliability:
Weak players = 90%*
Average players = 80%*
Strong players = 61%*

*NOTE: These percentages of reliability apply to the response of the player at which the information-gaining ploy is aimed.

Value Per Hour:
$1 limit = $3.30
$10 limit = $25.00
$100 limit = $171.00

Discussion: This is an extremely valuable maneuver. If the player continues or accelerates his bet in response to the faked calling motion, the pro will "reconsider" for a few seconds and then pass. If, however, the grab for calling chips causes the bettor to look back at his hand, there's an excellent chance that the bet is weak or an outright bluff.

If, after some hesitation, the player decides to go through with a bluff, he'll usually bet with extra emphasis as shown. This is an effort to appear strong (which means weak), so the pro will simply call and win the pot. If the player abandons his bet, that's also a big benefit for the pro. He will now win a pot on showdown when he wasn't prepared to call before his maneuver. On a few rare occasions, the player will double-check his hand for legitimate reasons. Then he'll come out betting rather sedately. This lack of force indicates one of the few times that a player who was made to hesitate really *did* have a strong hand. In such a case, the pro will pass.

Best Strategy: Use this technique only in the absence of other tells, because its overuse will wise up opponents and diminish the long-range effectiveness.

Photo by Raiko Hartman

Photo 107: The player at left is betting.

Photo by Raiko Hartman

Photo 108: In an effort to gain information, the expert at center reaches for his chips.

Photo by Raiko Hartman

Photo 109: This causes the bettor to take a second look at his cards.

Continued

Photo by Raiko Hartman

Photo 110: Now he completes the bet forcefully.

——————————— Photos 111, 112 & 113 ———————————

Title: You don't scare me.

Category: Gaining Information.

Description: Study the previous tell. This is the same maneuver, but the result is different. The bettor does not double-check his hand. Instead, he completes his bet with absolutely no hesitation.

Motivation: The pro is seeking to learn if the bettor is truly strong.

Reliability: Weak players = 90%*
                    Average players = 83%*
                    Strong players = 57%*

*NOTE: These percentages of reliability apply to the response of the player at which the information-gaining ploy is aimed.

Value Per Hour: $1 limit = $0.47
                    $10 limit = $3.50
                    $100 limit = $17.00

Discussion: The only difference between this and the tell we just studied is that the player isn't intimidated. The pro fails to make the opponent hesitate. This usually indicates strength, so passing is in order. Also notice that the bettor places his chips softly into the pot so as not to appear too strong. He really wants this call, but he's destined to be disappointed.

Best Strategy: This is the same maneuver as discussed in the previous tell. Remember not to overuse this strategy.

Photo 111: The player at left begins to bet.

Photo 112: The expert at center is using the same maneuver as in the previous tell.

Photo by Raiko Hartman

Photo 113: This time the player completes his bet without hesitation.

Chapter 23

Misdirected Bets

Any bet that challenges a secondary contender is a dead giveaway. It almost always means weakness.

If you had a strong hand, would you go out of your way to bet in a manner designed to challenge the player who was *least* likely to call? Of course not! If you wanted to challenge somebody, you'd go straight after the guy who's got a hand powerful enough to pay you off. That's simple sense. Bettors who violate that logic (by aiming their wager at or focusing their attention on someone who's scarcely a threat) are not having mental lapses. They are doing this by design, to make the strong hand feel that he is not even the real threat.

Don't you be fooled. When they bet, players with winning hands pay attention to their strongest-appearing opponents. If the most likely challenger is being ignored by the bettor, that's a bluff. Period.

It's too bad this kind of tell doesn't occur frequently; then it would be worth a great deal more money.

Caro's Law of Tells #23
A misdirected bet is almost always a bluff.

———————— Photo 114 ————————

Title: Why should aces scare me when I can beat this guy over here?

Category: Misdirected Bets.

Description: It seems like the player at left is going to a lot of trouble to bet past the man with these cards showing...

He's reaching clear across the table to challenge this...

Does that make sense to you?

Motivation: An attempt to make the stronger opponent feel insignificant in this pot.

Reliability: Weak players = 92%
              Average players = 87%
              Strong players = 84%

Value Per Hour: $1 limit = $0.65
              $10 limit = $4.04
              $100 limit = $22.80

Discussion: It seems reasonable that the man's hand at right contains garbage—possibly a failed straight. Ask yourself why the player would be reaching way across the table and betting into the weaker-looking of his two opponents. The answer is not very involved. This guy's bluffing. He probably holds something like a pair of kings.

Look at the expression of the man in the middle. He's thinking, and rightly so, "Hey, what about me? I'm in this pot, too!" Suppose you were the bettor and you wanted to be called. Say you had a hidden full house. Would you reach halfway to Cleveland to threaten a player who doesn't figure to call? Well, neither would this guy.

Best Strategy: Call as quickly as your fingers will allow.

Photo by Allen Photographers

Photo 114: This is seven stud. The player wearing the hat has a pair of aces showing, but the player on the right has truly ugly cards. So why is this bet being directed across the table?

205

Part Four

The Sounds of Tells

A long-time poker professional once said he could beat poker with his eyes closed. What he meant was that his opponents told him the strength of their hands just by the sounds they made.

He was not aware of the similar work I'd done which *Gambling Times* magazine had already published. When we compared notes, a few of his conclusions were the same as mine. However, he'd gone about his research in a very cumbersome fashion. Instead of using the basic tools of tell science—*weak means strong* and *strong means weak*—he had catalogued the things that people said and tried to uncover trends. He claimed that most of the things he heard had very little relevance to whether or not they were bluffing. But if they asked "How much is it to me?" and then raised, you could be pretty sure that they weren't bluffing.

That was a good conclusion. Players who ask for *any* clarification of the rules before they raise are legitimately strong. Often they already *know* the answer to their questions. By acting dumb, they're trying to convey that they're uncertain—that perhaps they'll raise or bet only if it doesn't cost too much. This is an *act* to appear weak and unsure. You should seldom call when a player asks, "How much is it to raise?"

Generally, it isn't the words your opponents choose as much as their tone of voice that gives you clues as to the strength of their hands. Anytime a player uses a sad tone, he or she is trying to feign weakness. Remember, pretended weakness means strength, so you should be cautious about calling sad tones. Especially cheerful tones are attempts to show contentment. Usually, these mean weakness.

Do you see how the sounds of tells follow the great principles of all other tell science? If a player is *acting,* whether it's by gesture or by voice, you should usually be persuaded to respond in a manner *opposite* of what he's trying to make you do.

If your opponent sounds threatening, figure him to be weak. If he sounds uncertain, figure him to be strong. If he sounds as if betting is misery, pass. If he chirps the words "I bet," as if his hand obviously merits a bet, call.

One of the great clues is the standard everyday sigh. When you hear an opponent sigh, he's trying to make you think he's disappointed. He isn't! Players sigh only if they hold strong hands. Any player who accompanies his bet with a sigh is performing the equivalent of shrugging his shoulders. In fact, you may encounter both the sigh and the shrug on the same wager. Both are intended to imply weakness or uncertainty. Both, in fact, mean strength and should seldom be called.

Often a player will sigh even before it's time to bet. This may happen when, for instance, he looks at the cards he's just drawn or sees the flop. Listen for that sigh, and when you hear it, beware.

Sometimes you'll meet a player who hums or whistles, usually quietly to himself or herself. This is *not* an act. Some players like to pass the time between hands in this manner. If the humming or whistling stops suddenly, you can be pretty sure the player just looked at a strong hand and intends to play. He is now concentrating.

The same is true of people who chatter continuously. When they are dealt a strong hand and intend to play, they must concentrate. At that time, their chatter will either cease or become erratic.

Keeping all this in mind, let's deal with one very important tell sound.

Do me a favor. Put your tongue on the inside edge of your teeth at the top of your mouth. Create some suction. Now withdraw your tongue briskly.

Did you hear that sound? Do it again. Again. Once more. Again.

I want you to remember that sound. It's a clack. I'm not sure that's a good definition, but it will have to do. No, on second thought, it *won't* have to do. Let's call it *Pokerclack* and that way we'll always know what we mean.

You'll hear Pokerclack fairly often in a game. Whenever you do, you must throw away any less-than-monster hand just as quickly as you are able. That's because you're usually going to hear this sound coming from an opponent who has an almost certain winner.

Remember, most weak to medium players tend to act weak when

they're strong. That's why it's usually bad policy to call a player who goes out of his way to sigh, shrug or act sad in any way.

Well, Pokerclack is a sad sound. Just to prove it, do this. Get ready to make Pokerclack. Put your tongue in the right position and apply suction.

Do not release Pokerclack.

Are you following instructions? Now suppose a friend walks up to you and says, "I just lost my whole month's pay at roulette."

Release Pokerclack now.

Aha! It sounded right, didn't it? It was an audible display of negativeness. Your friend would have interpreted it as such. It's as if you had said, "My-my, that's really too bad!"

But we know from previous tells that if a player goes out of his way to convey sorrow, he's probably got a winner. Therefore, a player making this sound at poker does *not* hold a bad hand.

Caro's Law of Tells #24
Beware of sighs and sounds of sorrow.

Caro's Law of Tells #25
Don't call Pokerclack.

Part Five

Important Tells Revisited

Now we're going to take another look at some important tells. You should use this section to refresh your memory and, perhaps, gain new insights before taking your final exam.

Photo by Cliff Stanley

Photo 115: Remember that players who stack their chips neatly are apt to play conservatively. The messy chips to the side are likely to represent this man's profit. He may play more liberally with those.

Photo 116: Again, expect this woman to play conservatively because her chips are neatly stacked. There's another tell at work here. It's seven stud and she's chosen to adjust her first three cards in an orderly fashion. If she's an experienced player, that probably doesn't mean much. But if she's a beginner, it probably hints that she's interested in playing this hand.

Photo by Allen Photographers

Photo 117: This player has bet and now decides to share his hand with a friend who's standing behind him. It's unlikely that he's bluffing.

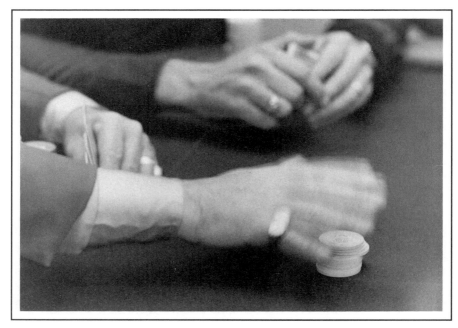

Photo by Frank Mitrani

Photo 118: Don't call that shaking hand. It's seldom a bluff.

Photo by Lee McDonald

Photo 119: Here's one of the most valuable tells in poker. First, this woman looks at her final card in seven stud...

Continued

217

Photo by Lee McDonald

Photo 120: Now she instantly and automatically glances at her chips. This means she likes her hand and intends to bet...

Photo 121: Quickly she looks away from her chips. If you were looking at your own hand when she glanced at her chips, you would have missed this profitable tell.

Photo by Amateur

Photo 122: Let's take another look at the glance-at-chips tell. This time it's draw poker and the player at right is asking for three cards.

Photo by Amateur

Photo 123: He picks up his three replacements, looks at them, and...

Photo by Amateur

Photo 124: Now he looks immediately to his chips. This glance will generally last less than a second, so if you're not watching your opponent, you'll miss it. When you see an opponent glance at his chips, you can be fairly sure he likes his hand and intends to bet.

Photo by Raiko Hartman

Photo 125: This is draw poker. The woman picks up the first three cards that have been dealt to her...

Photo by Raiko Hartman

Photo 126: She has securely transferred these to her left hand. Now she picks up the rest of her cards...

Photo by Raiko Hartman

Photo 127: She guards these and looks away from the action. Whenever you see a player guard cards, and then look away as if uninterested, you should expect a bet or a raise.

Photo by Allen Photographers

Photo 128: The woman is conspicuously looking away from the bettor and acting almost as if to pass. That combination usually means a raise is coming.

Photo by Frank Mitrani

Photo 129: It's hold 'em and this woman watches the flop...

Continued

225

Photo by Frank Mitrani

Photo 130: Seconds later she continues to study. This usually shows weakness, particularly among players who habitually look *away* when the flop pleases them.

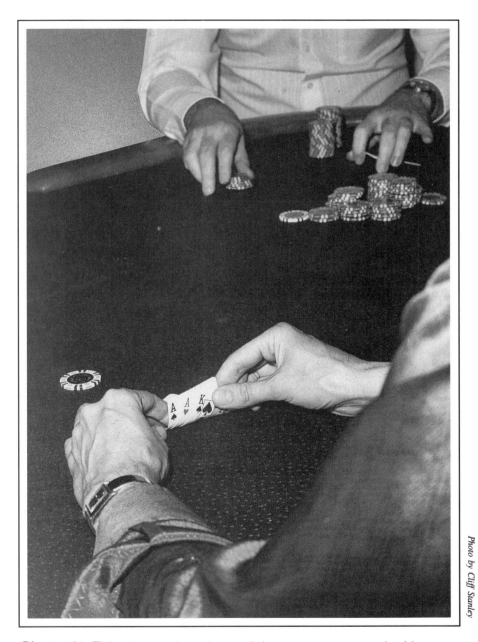

Photo by Cliff Stanley

Photo 131: This draw poker player picks up two aces and a king—a pretty powerful beginning...

Continued

227

Photo 132: Now he's secured these in his left hand and adds two dream cards, an ace and a king, giving him aces full...

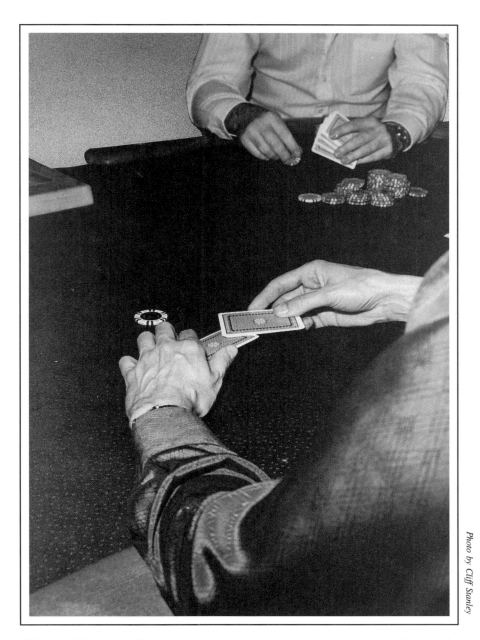

Photo 133: Immediately he puts these two new cards together with his first three...

Continued

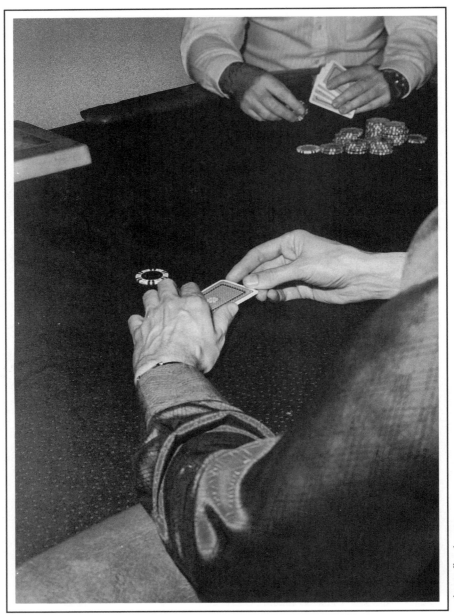

Photo by Cliff Stanley

Photo 134: And now he guards the whole hand. This tell can be contrasted to the common habit of continuing to stare at weak cards.

Photo 135: The player in the foreground is beginning to bet a marginal seven-stud hand. Judging by the player across the table, the wager is safe. When players stare at their cards in response to a coming bet, they're trying to discourage that bet. If this man held a strong hand, why would he want to prevent your bet?

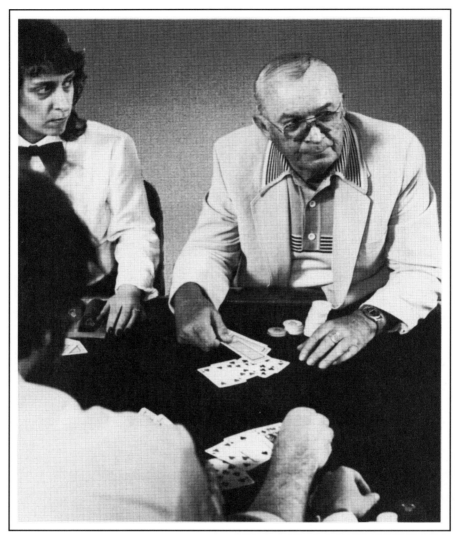

Photo by Lee McDonald

Photo 136: Compare this to the previous photo. The man in the foreground is again about to bet a marginal hand. This time his opponent looks away and pretends to be passing prematurely. This is always dangerous. Expect a raise.

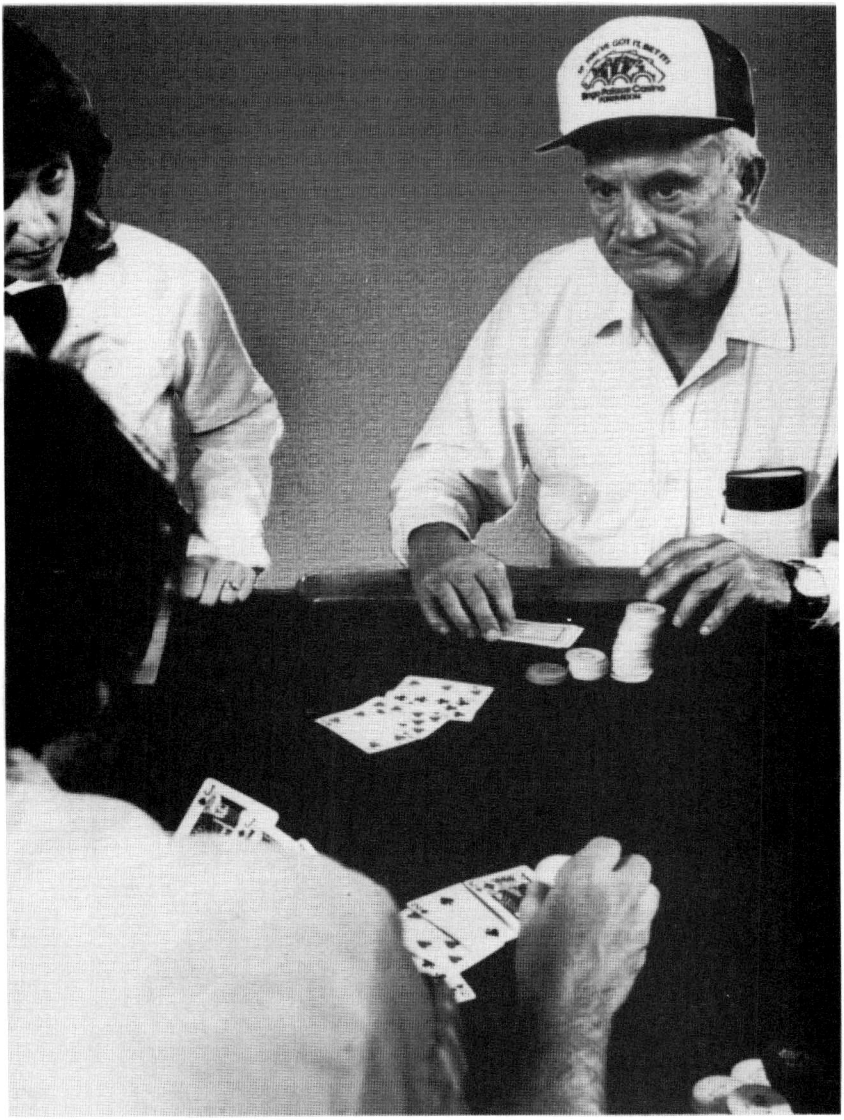

Photo by Lee McDonald

Photo 137: Here's another way a player might try to prevent the man in the foreground from betting. The man is staring at the bettor and reaching for his chips in a threatening manner. Remember, players who try to prevent your bets are weak and you should not be afraid to wager with medium-strength hands.

Photo by Lee McDonald

Photo 138: Any exaggerated betting move is likely to be a bluff. Here we see an unnaturally raised forearm.

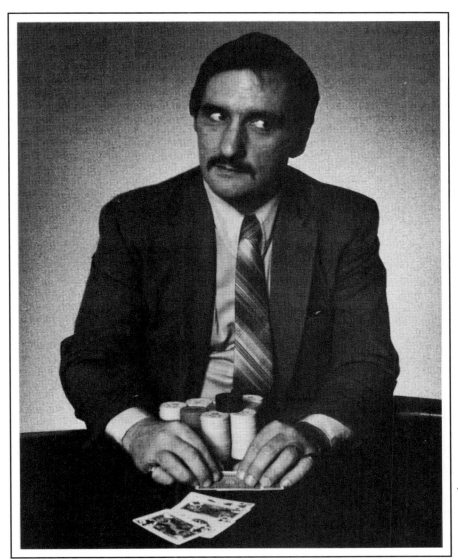

Photo by Frank Mitrani

Photo 139: If the head is turned away from the action, but the eyes are watching, beware. Don't be surprised if this man raises.

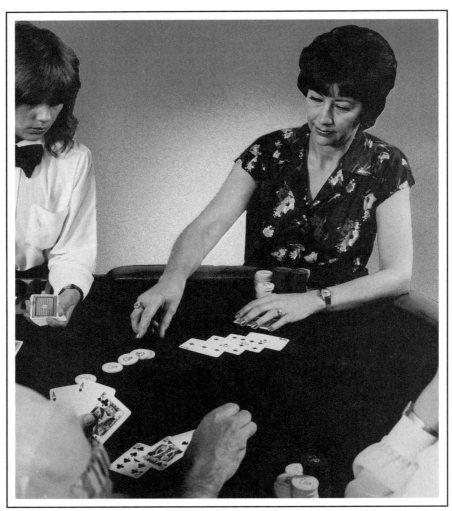

Photo by Lee McDonald

Photo 140: Sometimes you can determine whether or not an opponent is bluffing just by reaching for your chips. That's what the player is doing in the foreground as this woman bets. In response she shows no hesitation as she hurries to complete the bet. This means she has a strong hand.

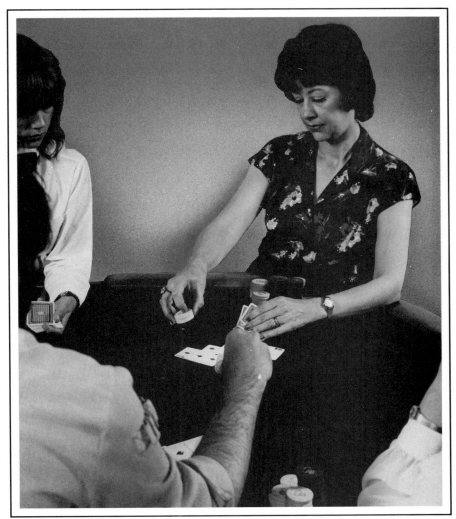

Photo by Lee McDonald

Photo 141: Take another look at the previous photo and compare it to this one. Here, again, the player in the foreground reaches for his chips as the woman wagers. This time she hesitates and looks back at her hand. If she completes this bet, particularly with extra force, there's a great chance that she's bluffing.

Photo by Frank Mitrani

Photo 142: The seven-stud player at center has just received a third card up and now he peeks at his hole cards. Always ask yourself why an opponent would be double-checking. Often, players know the *ranks* of their hole cards but not the suits. If, for instance, an opponent's board shows three suited cards and he checks his hole cards, he's searching for *one* more of that suit to provide a flush *opportunity*. He'd seldom have a flush already completed. It's unlikely that he'd need to double-check if he held *two* of the matching suit in the hole (although some players *do* double-check just in case their memory is tricking them). After a player who just caught a third suited card peeks into the hole, you should be less worried about his already-made flush.

Photo by Raiko Hartman

Photo 143: The seven-stud player at center is deliberately position-ing his bet to challenge a player who doesn't seem to be a threat. He's ignoring the woman with a pair of kings showing. Anytime a player *misdirects* a bet into a player who does not pose an apparent threat, you should suspect a bluff.

Part Six

Play Along Photo Quiz

Let's test what you've learned about tells. You'll find the answers near the end of this section, along with the chapters you should study if you made any mistakes.

Get ready, get nervous, go...

Photo by Raiko Hartman

Photo 144: *Question 1*— Judging by the way the player at left is taking his money from his wallet, do you expect him to play conservatively or liberally?

243

Photo 145: The seven-stud player at left is receiving his final card face down from the dealer...

Photo 146: Now he peeks at the card...

Photo by Frank Mitrani

Photo 147: This is his immediate reaction...

Photo by Frank Mitrani

Photo 148: ...Followed by this. *Question 2—* Would you bet a medium-strength hand into the player at left?

Photo 149: *Question 3—* Is the bettor at center bluffing?

Photo 150: You're the player in the left foreground. It's seven stud, all the cards have been dealt and you have two pair, jacks over sevens. Your opponent has a pair of tens on the board and three hearts. She checked before looking at her seventh card, but she now knows what it is. It's up to you. *Question 4—* Should you bet or check?

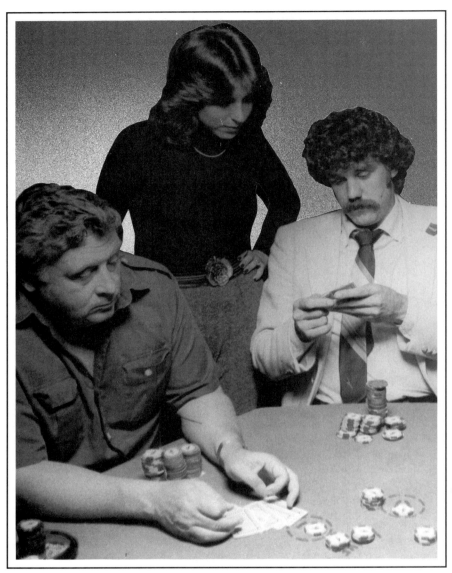

Photo 151: It's draw poker, after the draw. The player in the suit drew three cards and bet into you. You have two small pair. *Question 5—* Should you call, raise or pass?

Photo by Allen Photographers

Photo 152: The man standing is entering the game and buying chips. *Question 6—* Do you expect him to play conservatively or aggressively?

Photo by Lee McDonald

Photo 153: It's seven stud, six cards have been dealt and there's just one to come. The woman (center) has three hearts showing and is betting into the woman at right, who we'll say has only one pair. *Question 7—* If you were the woman at right, would you call this bet?

Photo by Lee McDonald

Photo 154: It's seven stud after all cards have been dealt. Your opponent is looking at his final card. He has four parts of a straight on
the board.

Continued

251

Photo 155: He is now aware of what his final card is.

Photo by Lee McDonald

Photo 156: You have queens up and check. *Question 8*—If this man bets, what should you do?

Photo 157: It's draw poker. The player second from right has opened in an early position and now requests three cards.

Photo 158: In response, his opponent (far right) asks for one card.

Photo by Raiko Hartman

Photo 159: *Question 9—* Study the player (right). Is he more likely to be drawing to a flush or to be holding two pair?

Photo 160: It's draw poker, jacks-or-better to open. The player second from left has opened and is taking three cards.

Photo 161: *Question 10—* Would you bet jacks up after he checked to you?

Photo by Frank Mitrani

Photo 162: It's five-card draw lowball. The man at left just decided to draw one card this very second. He had to make his decision while studying the frozen mannerisms of the player to his left. *Question 11—* How many cards will that player (second from left) probably draw?

257

Photo by Raiko Hartman

Photo 163: It's draw poker, jacks-or-better to open. The player at left has opened and is taking two. *Question 12—* What is the player more likely to have: A pair with a six kicker or three sixes?

Photo 164: Suppose you're in the left foreground with three aces. It's draw poker and it's your turn to act. *Question 13*— Should you open or is there another player who will bet for you?

Photo 165: It's draw poker and the woman is deciding how many to draw.

Photo 166: She needed two cards and now she looks at them.

Photo by Raiko Hartman

Photo 167: *Question 14—* Did the woman help her hand?

Photo by Frank Mitrani

Photo 168: Suppose you're playing seven stud and are seated to this player's right. You have aces up and are considering a bet. *Question 15—* Would your bet be safe?

Photo 169: The seven-stud player at left is making a bet. *Question 16*—Is the bet safe?

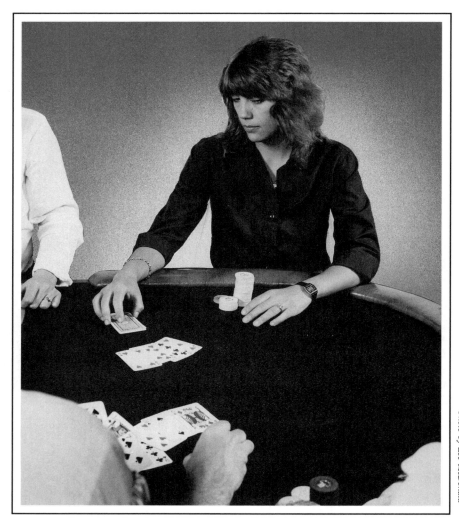

Photo by Lee McDonald

Photo 170: *Question 17—* Should you feel safe betting a medium-strong hand into this woman?

Photo by Frank Mitirani

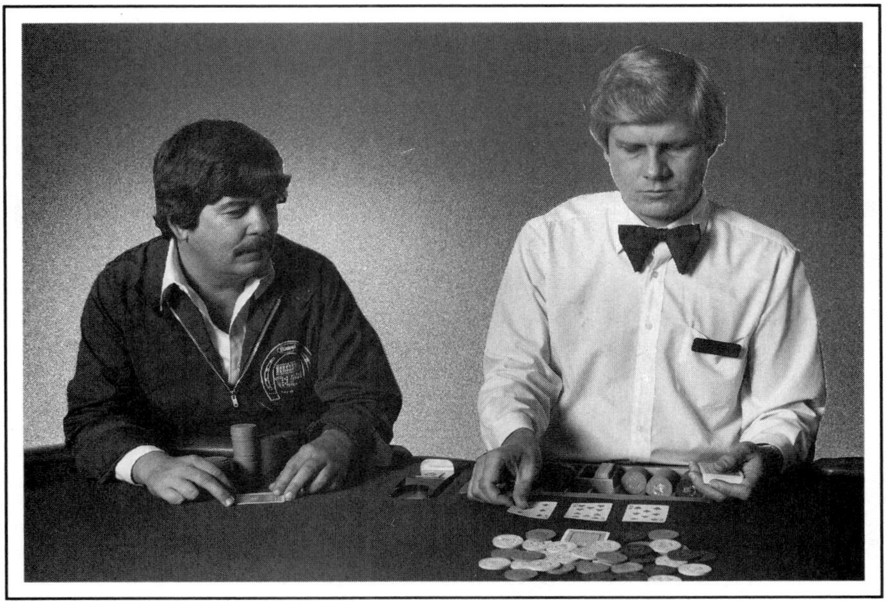

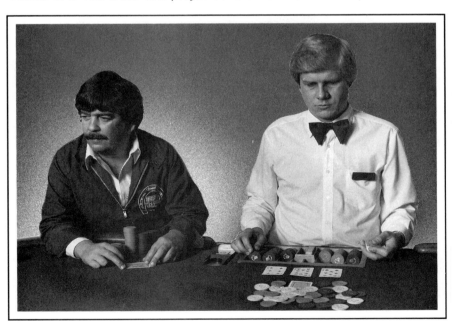

Photo 171: The hold 'em player at left watches the flop.

Photo by Frank Mitirani

Photo 172: *Question 18*— Did this player like the flop?

Photo 173: *Question 19*—Would you expect this player's basic game to be liberal or conservative? *Question 20*—Is he presently winning or losing?

Photo by Allen Photographers

Photo by Frank Mitrani

Photo 174: The player at right is beginning to bet. *Question 21—* Is the player at left going to pass?

Photo 175: It's after the draw. The player third from right opened and stood pat. He is now considering whether or not to bet his king-high straight. The woman in the black sweater called and drew one. *Question 22—* Should the man bet or check?

Photo by Lee McDonald

Photo 176: *Question 23*— You can choose the seat in the foreground or the one at the other end of the table. Which is better?

Photo Quiz Answers

Question 1: Conservatively. (Study Chapter 1, *Noncombat Tells,* page 3.)

Question 2: No, you shouldn't bet a medium-strength hand. (Study Chapter 7, *Glancing At Chips,* page 49 and Chapter 16, *Encouraging Your Bet,* page 147.)

Question 3: No, the shrugging bettor is not bluffing. (Study Chapter 12, *Weak Means Strong,* page 87.)

Question 4: You should check. The woman is looking away and pretending to pass. (Study Chapter 16, *Encouraging Your Bet,* page 147.)

Question 5: You should pass. (Study Chapter 2, *Sharing A Hand,* page 19.)

Question 6: The flamboyant manner in which he's buying his chips suggests he'll play aggressively. (Study Chapter 1, *Noncombat Tells,* page 3.)

Question 7: Yes, you should call this exaggerated bet. (Study Chapter 18, *Betting Moves,* page 159.)

Question 8: Pass. The opponent told you he made his hand when he looked briefly at his chips. (Study Chapter 7, *Glancing At Chips,* page 49.)

Question 9: He's more likely to be holding two pair. (Study Chapter 10, *Instant Reaction,* page 69.)

Question 10: Yes, you should bet jacks up. The player looked at three cards and checked instantly. (Study Chapter 10, *Instant Reaction,* page 69.)

Question 11: None. Players who act as if to draw cards out of turn frequently intend to "reconsider" and rap pat. (Study Chapter 12, *Weak Means Strong,* page 87.)

The following photo was taken immediately *after* the one used in this test question...

Photo by Frank Mitrani

Photo 177: The player second from left changes his mind and decides to rap pat. Also, see Photo 162 (page 257) to review what happened *before* this took place.

Question 12: A pair with a six kicker. (Study Chapter 14, *Exposing Cards,* page 137.)

Question 13: Don't open. The man in the sweater (third from right) will do it for you. (Study Chapter 15, *Opening Tells,* page 143.)

Question 14: No, she didn't help her hand. She's reaching for her chips threateningly. (Study Chapter 13, *Strong Means Weak,* page 117, and Chapter 17, *Discouraging Your Bet,* page 155.)

Question 15: No. The bet is dangerous. (Study Chapter 21, *Conflicting Tells,* page 185.)

Question 16: No. The bet is dangerous. The player at right is looking away and *acting* uninterested. (Study Chapter 12, *Weak Means Strong,* page 87.)

Question 17: No! Your bet is very dangerous. You must learn to recognize this tell. It is one of the most profitable and reliable in poker. (Study Chapter 12, *Weak Means Strong,* page 87, and Chapter 16, *Encouraging Your Bet,* page 147.)

Question 18: Yes, he liked the flop. He's looking away as if uninterested. (Study Chapter 12, *Weak Means Strong,* page 87.)

Question 19: Basically conservative. His main stacks of chips are neat. (Study Chapter 1, *Noncombat Tells,* page 3.)

Question 20: He's presently winning. The messy chips are his profits. (Study Chapter 1, *Noncombat Tells,* page 3.)

Question 21: Probably not. He's acting as if to throw his up card away, but he'll probably only readjust it. (Study Chapter 12, *Weak Means Strong,* page 87.)

Question 22: He should check. The woman is looking away. (Study Chapter 12, *Weak Means Strong,* page 87, and Chapter 16, *Encouraging Your Bet,* page 147.)

Question 23: The seat across the table is better. (Study Chapter 20, *Choosing Your Seat,* page 181.)

A Final Question

Photo by Lee McDonald

Photo 178: *Last question*—Would you feel safer betting into a player who looks like this...

Photo by Lee McDonald

Photo 179: . . .Or a player who looks like this?

* * *

If you don't know the answer to the final question, further study is suggested. I recommend *Mike Caro's Book of Tells*.

Caro's Laws of Tells
—A Summary

Here is a listing of all the Caro's Laws of Tells featured in this book. This convenient summary will serve as a quick reference guide to the general ideas involved in the tells you've just learned.

Caro's Great Law of Tells

Players are either acting or they aren't. If they are acting, then decide what they want you to do and disappoint them.

Caro's Law of Tells #1

Players often stack chips in a manner directly indicative of their style of play. Conservative means conservative; sloppy means sloppy.

Caro's Law of Tells #2

Players often buy chips in a manner directly indicative of their style of play. Flamboyant means flamboyant; guarded means guarded.

Caro's Law of Tells #3

Any unsophisticated player who bets, then shares his hand while awaiting a call, is unlikely to be bluffing.

Caro's Law of Tells #4

A trembling bet is a force to be feared.

Caro's Law of Tells #5

*In the absence of indications to the contrary,
call any bettor whose hand covers his mouth.*

Caro's Law of Tells #6

*A genuine smile usually means a genuine hand;
a forced smile is a bluff.*

Caro's Law of Tells #7

*The friendlier a bettor is,
the more apt he is to be bluffing.*

Caro's Law of Tells #8

*A player glances secretly at his chips only when
he's considering a bet—and almost always
because he's helped his hand.*

Caro's Law of Tells #9

*If a player looks and then checks instantly,
it's unlikely that he improved his hand.*

Caro's Law of Tells #10

*If a player looks and then bets instantly,
it's unlikely that he's bluffing.*

Caro's Law of Tells #11

Disappoint any player who,
by acting weak, is seeking your call.

Caro's Law of Tells #12

Disappoint any player who, by acting strong,
is hoping you'll pass.

Caro's Law of Tells #13

Players staring at you are usually less
of a threat than players staring away.

Caro's Law of Tells #14

Players staring at their cards are usually weak.

Caro's Law of Tells #15

Players reaching for their
chips out of turn are usually weak.

Caro's Law of Tells #16

A weak player who gathers a pot prematurely
is usually bluffing.

Caro's Law of Tells #17

When a player acts to spread his hand prematurely,
it's usually because he's bluffing.

Caro's Law of Tells #18

If a player bets and then looks back at his hand as you reach for your chips, he's probably bluffing.

Caro's Law of Tells #19

A forceful or exaggerated bet usually means weakness.

Caro's Law of Tells #20

A gentle bet usually means strength.

Caro's Law of Tells #21

When in doubt, sit behind the money.

Caro's Law of Tells #22

When tells conflict, the player is acting. Determine what he's trying to make you do by his most blatant mannerism. Then generally do the opposite.

Caro's Law of Tells #23

A misdirected bet is almost always a bluff.

Caro's Law of Tells #24

Beware of sighs and sounds of sorrow.

Caro's Law of Tells #25

Don't call Pokerclack.

KEEPING YOUR GAMING
KNOWLEDGE CURRENT

Now that you've read *The Book of Tells*, and know all about the Body Language of Poker, you'll want to keep abreast of the rapid and continuous changes and developments in this and other gaming fields. The best way to that is with a subscription to *Win* magazine.

Since February of 1977, readers of *Gambling Times* (now called *Win*) magazine have profited immensely. They have done so by using the information they have read each month. If that sounds like a simple solution to winning more and losing less, well it is!

Win is totally dedicated to showing readers how to win more money in every form of legalized gambling. How much you're going to win depends on many factors, but it's going to be considerably more than the cost of a subscription.

WINNING AND MONEY

Winning, that's what *Win* magazine is all about. And money, that's what *Win* is all about. Because winning and money go hand in hand.

Here's what the late Vince Lombardi, the famous football coach of the Green Bay Packers, had to say about winning:

> "It's not a sometime thing. Winning is a habit. There is no room for second place. There is only one place in my game and that is first place. I have finished second twice in my time at Green Bay and I don't ever want to finish second again. The objective is to win—fairly, squarely, decently, by the rules—but to win. To beat the other guy. Maybe that sounds hard or cruel. I don't think it is. It is and has always been an American zeal to be first in anything we do, and to win, and to win and to win."

Mr. Lombardi firmly believed that being a winner is "man's finest hour." *Win* believes it is too, while being a loser is depressing, ego-deflating, expensive and usually very lonely. "Everybody loves a winner" may be a cliché, but it's true. Winners command respect and are greatly admired. Winners are also very popular and have an abundance of friends. You may have seen a winner in a casino, with a bevy of girls surrounding him . . . or remember one who could get just about any girl he wanted.

Some of the greatest gamblers in the world also have strong views on what winning is all about. Here's what two of them have to say on the subject:

> "To be a winner, a man has to feel good about himself and know he has some kind of advantage going in. I never made bets on even chances. Smart is better than lucky."—"Titanic" Thompson

> "When it comes to winnin', I got me a one-track mind. You gotta want to win more than anything else. And you gotta have confidence. You can't pretend to have it. That's no good. You gotta have it. You gotta know. Guessers are losers. Gamblin's just as simple as that." —Johnny Moss

Win will bring you the knowledge you need to come home a winner and come home in the money. For it is knowledge, the kind of knowledge you'll get in its pages, that separates winners from losers. It's winning and money that *Win* offers you. *Win* will be your working manual to winning wealth.

The current distribution of this magazine is limited to selected newsstands in selected cities. Additionally, at newsstands where it is available, it's being snapped up, as soon as it's displayed, by gamblers who know a sure bet when they see one.

So if you're serious about winning, you're best off subscribing to *Win*. Then you can always count on its being there, conveniently delivered to your mailbox—and what's more, it will be there one or two weeks before it appears on the newsstands. You'll be among the first to receive the current issue as soon as it comes off the presses, and being first is the way to be a winner.

Having every monthly issue of *Win* will enable you to build an "Encyclopedia of Gambling," since the contents of this magazine are full of sound advice that will be as good in five or ten years as it is now.

As you can see, a subscription to *Win* is your best bet for a future of knowledgeable gambling. It's your ticket to *WINNING* and *MONEY*.

Take the time to read the following offer. *Win* has gone all out to give you outstanding bonuses. You can join the knowledgeable players who have learned that *Win* helps them to win more money.

 **SUBSCRIPTION BONUS OFFER**

We at **WIN**/Gambling Times have one goal: **To make you a more informed casino consumer**. The most profitable winning casino systems, the best hotel values, the finest in gambling resort dining and timely updates on the constantly-evolving international gaming scene—it's all in **WIN**, the mother of ALL gaming publications. NOW, you can receive 12 information-packed issues of **WIN** plus TWO exciting premiums from **WIN**'s Five-Point Subscription Bonus Plan. SUBSCRIBE NOW and we'll rush you **WIN**'s unbeatable **FREE** Gaming Vacation Package PLUS an additional premium of YOUR CHOICE! Don't miss out...**ACT NOW!**

Bonus #1
FREE Software

This is a collection of some of the finest freeware and shareware programs available. Blackjack and craps, roulette and baccarat, keno and lotto, greyhounds and thoroughbreds, sportsbetting and football pools.

Bonus #2
FREE Book

Select any book in our catalog marked Bonus Book **FREE**. Select from over 40 titles on over 10 different subjects. Remember, the better informed you are the better your game will be.

Bonus #3
FREE Booklets

A selection of some of the most informative booklets, pamphlets and brochures we have published. Including Nick the Greeks Crap System and our Gamblers Pocket Computer with a retail value of over $20. Quantities are limited so we are filling orders on a first come first served basis.

Bonus #4
FREE Blackjack Special

Take $10 off your Experts Blackjack. Newsletter subscription. That's 6 issues of the newsletter that anyone serious about blackjack should be reading. With articles geared to the advanced player and charts and reviews telling where the best games are AC, LV (Downtown & Strip), Reno, Tahoe, Laughlin, Mississippi and others!

To begin your delivery of *Win* magazine at once, enclose a payment of $44.00 by check or money order (U.S. currency), Master Card or Visa. Add ¢7.00 per year for postage outside the United States.

Send payment to:

> *WIN* MAGAZINE
> 16760 Stagg Street, #213
> Van Nuys, CA 91406

OTHER BOOKS AVAILABLE

If you can't find the following books at your local bookstore, they may be ordered directly from *Gambling Times*, 1018 N. Cole Ave., Hollywood, CA 90038. Information on how to order is on page 294.

Poker Books

According to Doyle by Doyle Brunson—Acknowledged by most people as the world's best all-around poker player, twice World Champion Doyle Brunson brings you his homespun wisdom from over 30 years as a professional poker player. This book will not only show you how to win at poker, it will give you valuable insights into how to better handle that poker game called LIFE. Softbound. $6.95. (ISBN: 0-89746-003-0)

Poker for Women by Mike Caro—How women can take advantage of the special male-female ego wars at the poker table and win. This book also has non-poker everyday value for women. Men can be destroyed at the poker table by coy, cunning or aggressive women. That's because, on a subconscious level, men expect women to act traditionally. This book tells women when to flirt, when to be tough and when to whimper. Many of the tactics are tried and proven by Caro's own students. This book does not claim that women are better players, merely that there are strategies available to them that are not available to their male opponents. Softbound. $5.95. (ISBN: 0-89746-009-X)

Wins, Places, and Pros by Tex Sheahan—With more than 50 years of experience as a professional poker player and cardroom manager/tournament director, Tex lets his readers in on the secrets that separate the men from the boys at the poker table. Descriptions of poker events, playing experiences from all over the world, and those special personalities who are the masters of the game. . .Tex knows them all and lays it out in his marvelous easy-to-read style. Softbound. $6.95. (ISBN: 0-89746-008-1)

Free Money: How to Win in the Cardrooms of California by Michael Wiesenberg— Computer expert and poker writer par excellence, Michael Wiesenberg delivers critical knowledge to those who play in the poker rooms of the western states. Wiesenberg gives you the precise meaning of the rules as well as the mathematics of poker to aid public and private poker players alike. Wiesenberg, a prolific author, is published by more gaming periodicals than any other writer. Softbound. $8.95. (ISBN: 0-89746-027-8)

The Railbird by Rex Jones—The ultimate kibitzer, the man who watches from the rail in the poker room, has unique insights into the character and performance of all poker players. From this vantage point, Rex Jones, Ph.D., blends his expertise and considerable education in anthropology with his lifetime of poker playing and watching. The result is a delightful book with exceptional values for those who want to avoid the fatal errors of bad players and capitalize upon the qualities that make up the winning strengths of outstanding poker players. Softbound. $6.95. (ISBN: 0-89746-028-6)

Tales Out of Tulsa by Bobby Baldwin—Oklahoma-born Bobby Baldwin, the youngest player to ever win the World Championship of Poker, is considered to be among the top five poker players in the world. Known affectionately as "The Owl," this brilliant poker genius, wise beyond his years, brings the benefits of his experience to the pages of this book. It's sure to stop the leaks in your poker game, and you will be amazingly ahead of your opponents in the very next game you play. Softbound. $6.95. (ISBN: 0-89746-006-5)

Blackjack Books

The Beginner's Guide to Winning Blackjack by Stanley Roberts—The world's leading blackjack writer shows beginners to the game how to obtain an instant advantage through the simplest of techniques. Covering Basic Strategy for all major casino areas from Las Vegas to the Bahamas, Atlantic City and Reno/Tahoe, Roberts provides a simple system to immediately know when the remaining cards favor the player. The entire method can be learned in less than two hours and taken to the casinos to produce sure profits.
Softbound. $10.00. (ISBN: 0-89746-014-6)

The Gambling Times Guide to Blackjack by Stanley Roberts with Edward O. Thorp, Ken Uston, Lance Humble, Arnold Snyder, Julian Braun, D. Howard Mitchell, Jerry Patterson, and other experts in this field—The top blackjack authorities have been brought together for the first time to bring to the reader the ins and outs of the game of blackjack. All aspects of the game are discussed. Winning techniques are presented for beginners and casual players.
Softbound. $9.95. (ISBN: 0-89746-015-4)

Million Dollar Blackjack by Ken Uston—Every blackjack enthusiast or gaming traveler who fancies himself a "21" player can improve his game with this explosive bestseller. Ken Uston shows you how he and his team won over 4 million dollars at blackjack. Now, for the first time, you can find out how he did it and how his system can help you. Includes playing and betting strategies, winning secrets, protection from cheaters, Uston's Advanced Point Count System, and a glossary of inside terms used by professionals.
Hardbound. $16.95.(ISBN: 0-914314-08-4)

Casino Games

The Gambling Times Guide to Casino Games by Len Miller—The co-founder and editor of *Gambling Times* magazine vividly describes the casino games and explains their rules and betting procedures. This easy-to-follow guide covers blackjack, craps, roulette, keno, video machines, progressive slots and more. After reading this book, you'll play like a pro!
Softbound. $9.95. (ISBN: 0-89746-017-0)

The Gambling Times Guide to Craps by N.B. Winkless, Jr.—The ultimate craps book for beginners and experts alike. It provides you with a program to tackle the house edge that can be used on a home computer. This text shows you which bets to avoid and tells you the difference between craps in Nevada and craps in other gaming resort areas. It includes a glossary of terms and a directory of dealer schools.
Softbound. $9.95. (ISBN: 0-89746-013-8)

General Interest Books

Caro on Gambling by Mike Caro—The world's leading poker writer covers all the aspects of gambling from his regular columns in *Gambling Times* magazine and *Poker Player* newspaper. Discussing odds and probabilities, bluffing and raising, psychology and character, this book will bring to light valuable concepts that can be turned into instant profits in home games as well as in the poker palaces of the West.
Softbound. $6.95. (ISBN: 0-89746-029-4)

The Gambling Times Guide to Systems That Win, Volume I and Volume II—For those who want to broaden their gambling knowledge, this two-volume set offers complete gambling systems used by the experts. Learn their strategies and how to incorporate them into your gambling style. **Volume I** covers 12 systems that win for roulette, craps, backgammon, slot machines, horse racing, baseball, basketball and football.
Softbound. $5.95. (ISBN: 0-89746-034-0)
Volume II features 12 more systems that win, covering horse racing, craps, blackjack, slot machines, jai alai and baseball.
Softbound. $5.95. (ISBN: 0-89746-034-0)

The Gambling Times Guide to Winning Systems, Volume I and Volume II—For those who take their gambling seriously, *Gambling Times* presents a two-volume set of proven winning systems. Learn how the experts beat the house edge and become consistent winners. **Volume I** contains 12 complete strategies for casino games and sports wagering, including baccarat, blackjack, keno, basketball and harness handicapping.
Softbound. $5.95. (ISBN: 0-89746-032-4)
Volume II contains 12 more winning systems covering poker bluffing, pitching analysis, greyhound handicapping and roulette.
Softbound. $5.95. (ISBN: 0-89746-033-2)

The Mathematics of Gambling by Edward O. Thorp—The "Albert Einstein of gambling" presents his second book on the subject. His first book, *Beat The Dealer,* set the gambling world on its heels and struck fear into the cold-blooded hearts of Las Vegas casino-owners in 1962. Now, more than twenty years later, Dr. Thorp again challenges the odds by bringing out a simple to understand version of more than thirty years of exploration into all aspects of what separates winners from losers...knowing the real meaning of the parameters of the games.
Softbound. $7.95. (ISBN: 0-89746-019-7)

P$yching Out Vegas by Marvin Karlins, Ph.D.—The dream merchants who build and operate gaming resorts subtly work on the casino patron to direct his attention, control his actions and turn his pockets inside out. At last, their techniques are revealed to you by a noted psychologist who shows you how you can successfully control your behavior and turn a losing attitude into a lifetime winning streak.
Hardbound. $15.00. (ISBN: 0-914314-03-3)

Winning by Computer by Dr. Donald Sullivan—Now, for the first time, the wonders of computer technology are harnessed for the gambler. Dr. Sullivan explains how to figure the odds and identify key factors in all forms of race and sports handicapping.
Softbound. $5.95. (ISBN: 0-89746-018-9)

The Gambling Times Quiz Book by Mike Caro—Learn while testing your knowledge. Caro's book includes questions and answers on the concepts and information published in previous issues of *Gambling Times*. Caro tells why an answer is correct and credit is given to the author whose *Gambling Times* article suggested the question. This book covers only established fact, not the personal opinions of authors, and Caro's inimitable style makes this an easy-reading, easy-learning book.
Softbound. $5.95. (ISBN: 0-89746-031-6)

How to Win at Gaming Tournaments by Haven Earle Haley—Win your share of the millions of dollars and fabulous prizes being awarded to gaming contestants, and have the glory of being a World Champion. Poker, gin rummy, backgammon, craps, blackjack and baccarat are all popular tournament games. The rules, special tournament regulations, playing procedures, and how to obtain free entry are fully explained in this informative manual. The tournament promoters—who they are, where they hold events—and the cash and prizes awarded are explained in detail. Tournament play usually requires special strategy changes, which are detailed in this book.
Softbound. $8.95. (ISBN: 0-89746-016-2)

Sports Betting Books

Fast Track to Thoroughbred Profits by Mark Cramer—A unique approach to selecting winners, with price in mind, by distinguishing between valuable and commonplace information. Results: higher average pay-offs and solid flat bet profits. How to spot signs of improvement and when to cash in. And much, much more.
Softbound. $6.95. (ISBN: 0-89746-025-1)

The Gambling Times Guide to Basketball Handicapping by Barbara Nathan—This easy-to-read, highly informative book is the definitive guide to basketball betting. Expert sports handicapper Barbara Nathan provides handicapping knowledge, insightful coverage, and step-by-step guidance for money management. The advantages and disadvantages of relying on sports services are also covered.
Softbound. $5.95. (ISBN: 0-89746-023-5)

The Gambling Times Guide to Football Handicapping by Bob McCune—Starting with the novice's approach to handicapping football, and winding up with some of the more sophisticated team selection techniques in the sports handicapping realm, this book will actually tell the reader how to forecast, *in advance,* the final scores of most major national football games. The author's background and expertise on the subject will put money into any sports gambler's pocket.
Softbound. $5.95. (ISBN: 0-89746-022-7)

The Gambling Times Guide to Greyhound Racing by William E. McBride—This complete discussion of greyhound racing is a must for anyone who is just beginning to appreciate this exciting and profitable sport. The book begins with a brief overview detailing the origins of greyhound racing and pari-mutuel betting, and explains the greyhound track environment, betting procedures, and handicapping methods. Includes an appendix of various greyhound organizations, a review of greyhound books, and an interesting section on famous dogs and personalities in the world of greyhound racing.
Softbound. $9.95. (ISBN: 0-89746-007-3)

The Gambling Times Guide to Harness Racing by Igor Kusyshyn, Ph.D., Al Stanley and Sam Dragich—Three of Canada's top harness handicapping authorities present their inside approach to analyzing the harness racing scene and selecting winners. All the important factors from the type of sulky, workouts, drivers' ratings, speed, pace, etc., are skillfully presented in simple terms that can be used by novices and experienced racegoers to find the likely winners.
Softbound. $5.95. (ISBN: 0-89746-002-2)

The Gambling Times Guide to Jai Alai by William R. Keevers—The most comprehensive book on jai alai available. Author Bill Keevers takes the reader on an informative journey from the ancient beginnings of the game to its current popularity. This easy-to-understand guide will show you the fine points of the game, how to improve your betting percentage, and where to find jai alai frontons.
Softbound. $5.95. (ISBN: 0-89746-010-3)

The Gambling Times Guide to Thoroughbred Racing by R.G. Denis—Newcomers to the racetrack and veterans alike will appreciate the informative description of the thoroughbred pari-mutuel activity supplied by this experienced racing authority. Activities at the track and available information are blended skillfully in this guide to selecting winners that pay off in big-ticket returns.
Softbound. $5.95. (ISBN: 0-89746-005-7)

Ordering Information

Send your book order along with your check or money order to:

Gambling Times
16760 Stagg Street, #213
Van Nuys, CA 91406

Softbound Books: Please add $2.00 per book if delivered in the United States, $2.50 in Canada or Mexico, and $3.50 for foreign countries.
Hardbound books: Shipping charges for the following books are $2.50 if delivered in the United States, $3.00 in Canada or Mexico, and $5.00 for foreign countries:
Million Dollar Blackjack
P$yching Out Vegas